P9-ARQ-960

HELEN M. STEVENS'
EMBROIDERED FLOWERS

David & Charles

Trafalgar Square Publishing

For my Mother

*The plates shown on pages 1–3
illustrate some of the ways in
which flowers and foliage may
be used in embroidery, whether
capturing favourite blooms,
embellishing a more stylised
design, or to simply cover the
canvas.*

Title page: PLATE 1
8.25 x 9.5cm (3¼ x 3¾in)
This page above: PLATE 2
9 x 12.75cm (3½ x 5in)
Above right: PLATE 3
17 x 11.5cm (6¾ x 4½in)
Opposite page: PLATE 4
16 x 26cm (6¼ x 10¼in)

A DAVID & CHARLES BOOK

First published in 2000
Text and designs Copyright © Helen M. Stevens 2000
Photography and layout Copyright © David & Charles 2000

Printed in Hong Kong by Sino Publishing Ltd.

Helen M. Stevens has asserted her right to be identified as author of this work
in accordance with the Copyright, Designs and Patents Act, 1988.

First published in the UK in 2000 by David & Charles Publishers,
Brunel House, Newton Abbot, Devon
ISBN 0 7153 0995 1

First published in United States of America in 2000 by
Trafalgar Square Publishing,
North Pomfret, Vermont 05053, USA
ISBN 1-57076-171-X

A catalogue record for this book is available from the British Library.

Photography by Nigel Salmon
Book design by Margaret Foster

CONTENTS

INTRODUCTION 4

CHAPTER ONE
FIELDS AND MEADOWS 9

CHAPTER TWO
THE COTTAGE GARDEN 25

CHAPTER THREE
WAYSIDES 41

CHAPTER FOUR
WOODLAND GLADES 57

CHAPTER FIVE
THE RIVERSIDE 73

MATERIALS 88

BASIC TECHNIQUES 90

STITCH VARIATIONS 92

SUPPLIERS 95

ACKNOWLEDGEMENTS 95

INDEX 96

INTRODUCTION

Flowers and embroidery have flourished as close bedfellows since the earliest recorded textile designs. Their intimacy is not surprising since the diversity of shape, colour and habit in the realm of flowers offers infinite variety and inspiration to the artist in any media, and embroidery with its choice of texture, technique and application rises to the challenge of floral interpretation on many levels.

Whether naturalistic or stylised, flowers and their associated foliage suggest endless combinations of subject matter, concentrating specifically upon themselves or in conjunction with other motifs. They can be the focal point of a study or the framework within which another subject is set, as can be seen by the varied colour Plates 1 to 5. They can form the foreground of a landscape or the backdrop for a close-up portrait. They can subtly enhance a dramatic, narrative embroidery or riot unchecked across a whole canvas, revelling in their own unique characteristics.

During the mid-eighteenth century so popular was the embroidery of flowers that the terms 'to embroider' and 'to flower' became interchangeable. Fashions, of course, alter and over the centuries embroiderers' choice of flowers in their work has often reflected the preoccupations of the age. In the Middle Ages, their symbolism was an important factor – the lily representing the Virgin was a popular motif. Later, the Tudor rose was an emblem of power and majesty. Plants and flowers which were included in Herbals and Bestiaries found their way into embroidery design. As new worlds opened up, strange, exotic blooms entered the genre – Paisleys inspired by eastern textiles hybridised with western floral motifs to create strange, surreal effects, and Art Deco designs simplified flowers into striking arcs and ziggurats of pure colour. Some motifs have survived almost unchanged through millennia – the classical acanthus still provides an elegant and useful device to decorate the corner of a formal composition. Throughout history, the art of embroidery coupled with a love of flowers has proved an enduring bond.

This unique partnership is one to be cherished and enjoyed and, as a choice of subject matter, can be as simple or a complex as your confidence allows. In this book, I aim to dispel the myth that designing your own work and embroidering from nature need be an intimidating prospect. This is achieved by getting to know the structure and habits of individual flowers and understanding the ways in which they relate to each other, their surroundings and, more importantly from a practical viewpoint, how they best allow realistic interpretation through embroidery.

BASIC PLANT ANATOMY

Observation is the most useful tool in any workbox; without it, the finest needles, the most vibrant threads, can only achieve superficial results. Although no colours seem to 'clash' in a natural setting (bright red poppies and mauve mallows create an unexpected harmony rather than a jarring discord), an obviously ill-matched combination of subjects will not 'work'. It is important to understand how and why certain flowers grow together, what makes their habitats special and the fundamental structures of their flowers. The frilly, tissue-paper petals of the sweet peas in your garden might seem an impossibly complex project until you understand that this typical pea flower, with its upper and lower lobes, varies very little from the

◄ *PLATE 5*

There is always colour and inspiration to be found in nature: every season sports its own flowers if you know where to look. Here, clockwise from the bottom, plants intertwine to create the endless cycle of the seasons. The bright yellow winter aconite (Eranthis hymalis) *gives way to ivy* (Hedera helix) *and the delicate white snowdrop* (Galanthus nivalis). *The sweet violet* (Viola odorata) *leads to the dog roses* (Rosa canina) *of high summer and white bryony* (Bryonia dioica) *of autumn. Holly* (Ilex aquifolium), *with its scarlet berries, brings us back to winter once again.*

23 x 23cm (9 x 9in)

elementary vetch (see Fig 1). Its shape allows only certain insects access to nectar and pollen, and its tendrils are strategically placed to provide optimum support. Become familiar with one member of the family and the mystery of many others immediately lessens.

The Masterclass project at the end of each chapter explores the embroidery of various types of flowers in great detail. To choose the appropriate stitch techniques for each flower and its many component parts it is necessary to understand the anatomy of the plants themselves. To appreciate why certain flowers have delicate traceries leading the eye into its pollen-filled centre or have tightly pursed lips which can only be prised apart by heavy insects, is invaluable when choosing thread textures and gauges.

The function of all flowers is reproduction and Fig 2 shows all the features of a typical flowering plant which allow it to achieve this. Usually, a flower consists of several sepals forming the calyx on the outside of the bloom, petals (varying in number and shape, but generally colourful), stamens which produce the flower's pollen, and one or more carpels from which the fruits and seeds will develop. These four basic features appear in a wide variety of forms and an understanding of their respective names and relationships to each other helps in interpreting specific flowers. Seeds develop when pollen of the right type touches the stigma on top of the carpel. This is pollination and brightly coloured petals and intricate patterns are intended to lure bees and other insects into the flower to ensure that it takes place

◀ FIG 1

The flower of the garden sweet pea (left) comprises three layers of petals: topmost is the posterior petal (1), beneath it are the lateral petals (2) and, supported by the calyx (4) is the keel (3), which is formed from the two anterior petals, fused to create a boat-like structure. The wild vetch (right) is similar in structure.

FIG 2 ▶

A typical (imaginary!) flowering plant shows all its component parts. The flower, shown in more detail to the left, and bud (1 and 2) crown the plant, supported by the flower stalk (3). A bract (4), emerges from the stem (8) to support the flower, and a stipule (7) emerges beneath the leaf stalk (6) or petiole, which supports the leaf (5). The root (9) is rarely visible.

On the flower, the petals (1) are supported by the sepals which form the calyx (2) protecting the reproductive organs which include the stamens and anthers (3 and 5) and the carpel, stigma and style (4, 6 and 7). Becoming familiar with the names of these parts of the plant will help in interpreting the directions accompanying the Masterclass projects.

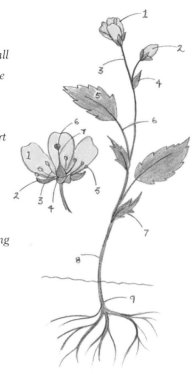

(although it may also been effected by the wind). Stems and leaves also comprise specific features which need to be identified if we are to describe them accurately. Leaves may be single or compound. Compound leaves are formed by a number of distinct leaflets, bracts emerge at the base of flower stalks and stipules are tiny leaves at the base of leaves or their stems.

WORKING THE MASTERCLASSES

Beginning with simple structures and progressing to more complex shapes, the Masterclass projects offer an opportunity to become familiar with how the component parts of flowers can be approached individually, separating complicated subjects into their elementary parts. The various stages of the embroidery are accompanied by stepped instructions and detailed photographs, close-ups of the actual stitching. Some of the close-ups may show elements stitched that have yet to be described – just follow the steps to keep in sequence. All the stitch variations used and the basic techniques needed to prepare your work are described at the back of the book. There is advice on choosing fabric and threads and making the most of your materials, and also how to mount and display completed embroideries.

Most of the embroideries shown in this book are worked in silk. Floss silks have a high sheen which is particularly attractive when worked in the techniques described – directional stitching which catches the light and reflects it to give a three-dimensional effect. However, untwisted silk is not to everyone's taste. Many enthusiasts prefer the subtler glow created by twisted silks, or by stranded embroidery cottons. All the techniques described in the Masterclasses are equally well suited to either choice and there is advice with regard to threads and fabrics in Materials, page 88.

A completed Masterclass should reflect personal preferences, rather than be a slavish copy! After all, there are no absolute constants in nature. No two flowers are identical, no two sunny afternoons reveal the same flowers juxtaposed indistinguishably from one day to the next. Soils vary, nutrients reaching the plants affect their flowers, cross-pollination results in subtly different shades and markings, on petals and leaves (see Fig 3). Within twenty-four hours the sun can fade a pillar-box red poppy to a rusty, red-brick orange. Leaves darken as the season progresses and a plant approaches maturity, berries ripen from yellow-green to crimson in a few hot days. To reflect the living, changing face of nature the choice of colours for completing the Masterclasses has not been set in stone.

Colour charts accompanying each project are shaded similarly to the pencil sketches elsewhere in the book. Each colour has been identified by a number and given a representative name but the specific choice of thread and colour has been left to you. In this way, as your confidence grows, you can experiment with different colourways. As long as a shade is identified by its number, its designation as 'red' or 'yellow' can be changed to 'orange' or 'white'. If the chosen shades are suitable alternatives, given the species of the subject, the scope for creating a unique piece of work is wide. Once you are happy with the techniques as explained in the Masterclasses themselves, the other coloured pencil sketches throughout the book can be used as patterns, either singly, combined, or with various elements extrapolated and enlarged.

Preparing this book has been a revelation in a number of ways. The research on the subject matter has reinforced my love of the countryside, and made me realise just how many of the 'weeds' once taken for granted or even persecuted are now rare and precious. However tempted you may be, *never* pick wildflowers and bring them back to your drawing board: sketch from life, or take a photo. In its natural surroundings a wildflower is, in any case, a much better subject.

I have also seen my own garden in a new light. Familiar flowers have revealed both their simplicity and complexities in surprising ways. Of course, these can be picked, sketched and stitched from life – even dissected to achieve a real understanding of a flower's anatomy. Lying full length on the lawn, I thought I knew what an antirrhinum looked like until I opened its soft, velvety mouth with my little finger, only to reveal an angry bumble bee, interrupted at his labours!

In describing and working the Masterclasses I also realised that many of the techniques which I have come to use every day over the last twenty years have become second nature. 'Seeing' the light and how it plays on a subject, and interpreting those effects through shadow lining, sweeping directional stitches and changes of texture is an ability which, once mastered, changes your perception and approach to embroidery for ever.

Helen M. Stevens' Embroidered Flowers is an extension of my own sketch pad and tambour hoop – I offer it to you as a source of inspiration and enjoyment. Share my techniques as you wish, incorporate your own ideas and interpret mine. Remember that every embroidery – yours and mine – is unique, a source of fulfilment and pleasure, and as individual as each flower is beautiful.

FIG 3 ▶

Both antirrhinum and honeysuckle have evolved to invite pollination by large insects, such as bumble bees.

CHAPTER ONE

FIELDS AND MEADOWS

Imagine a balmy summer afternoon: warm sun, gentle breeze, birds singing, the lazy humming of bumble

bees and the heady smell of hay and sweet herbs. Every sense is stimulated. Above all, the eye is

charmed and dazzled by the shimmering variety of sun-drenched flowers. Arable fields, grazing pastures

and meadows are home to an amazing diversity of wildflowers, differing, each to its own favoured

habitat, but often sharing a love of open spaces and accessibility to the sun.

The plants which thrive on regularly ploughed land – today often large, rolling fields given over to the production of cereal crops – are generally annuals. Their seeds require light to germinate and the seasonal tilling of the soil fulfils this need. When fields were smaller and less tightly controlled by the use of herbicides these species often turned whole cornfields red, blue or yellow as great swathes of poppies, cornflowers and corn marigolds embroidered the canvas of the countryside. Improved standards of crop purity have in places eliminated these spectacular plants, but where less rigid farming regimes are applied it is still possible to be charmed by their brash brilliance.

Meadows and hayfields yield different floral displays. Meadow thistles and buttercups, perennial plants with gentler, pastel shaded flowers, generally survive well in regularly grazed fields, as they are distasteful to cattle, whilst red clover is treated as a valuable addition to the hay crop, both as extra fodder and for its ability to enrich the soil with nitrogen.

White or Dutch clover is encouraged by bee keepers as its sweet smelling, abundant nectar can only be reached by long-tongued insects such as honey bees. Many other

◀ *PLATE 6*

The essence of farmland is captured in rolling fields, lush meadows and a scattering of wildflowers creating a foreground and framework. The scene is carefully set within boundaries, the formal composition complemented by the fluid lines of the flowers framing it.

Corn marigolds (Chrysanthemum segetum), far right, were once so common that they seriously compromised arable crops, but have now almost completely succumbed to herbicides in many areas. Where they survive, however, they are a joy to behold and live up to their country name of 'sunshine daisies'.

23 x 21.5cm (9 x 8½in)

▲ *FIG 4*

Lucerne and clover are important food plants for both bumble bees and hive-dwelling honey bees (shown here). If a design such as this is traced and transferred onto fabric ready for embroidery, take particular care to include all the details of the flower heads. The structure of the individual florets needs to be fully evident on the fabric to convey the detail successfully.

delicate members of the pea family, such as spotted medick and lucerne, occasionally colonise the borders of fields where once they might have been grown as crops.

The pea family is one of the largest in the plant kingdom. Used by mankind since the earliest of times, both truly wild and naturalised species are abundant in pasture land. To the left of the study in Plate 6, purple lucerne (*Medicago sativa*) intertwines with spotted medick (*Medicago arabica*). The medicago which gives medick its common name (once shared with lucerne) does not refer to medicine, but means 'plant of the Medes' an ancient civilisation of Persia, where it was widely cultivated. The name was given to both plants by the Romans, who probably introduced lucerne to Britain as a foodstuff for their animals. Red clover (*Trifolium pratense*), bottom right, has also been widely cultivated as animal fodder and is an important food plant for the increasingly rare bumble bee. It is affectionately known in many country areas as 'bee-bread'. Other uses include the making of a syrup to treat whooping cough, and a heady country wine.

Many smaller bloomed flowers, including the clovers and lucerne, have complicated structures and Fig 4 explores these in further detail. Lucerne is most often purple, but its flowers may occasionally be yellow or, rarely, green. It shares the typical trefoil 'clover leaf' foliage – a popular motif in embroidery since the earliest of times – with its cousins the red and white clover, though each are significantly different. Lucerne's leaves emerge from a spur on the stem of the plant and are toothed toward their tip. Red clover is smooth and ovate, whilst white clover (*Trifolium repens*) sports the traditional shamrock-shaped leaves, both with a V-shaped paler band running across their middle. A host of country superstitions surround the family, the best known being the hunting of the elusive four-leafed clover, originally worn to ward off witches and warlocks, now the symbol of good luck.

Field headlands, the uncultivated strips which surround many modern fields, can retain patches of a seed bank suggesting other small flowers which once rioted at their centre (Fig 5). These represent 'natural history' in its truest sense, giving us a glimpse of past landscapes and practices. In Plate 7 the corncockle and cornflower suggest that the

◀ *PLATE 7*

Whilst field poppies (Papaver rhoeas) *are still relatively common, two flowers which once also painted the cornfields are now rare: the rich blue cornflower* (Centaurea cyanus) *and the striking pink corncockle* (Agrostemma githago)*.*

The country name of the cornflower is the 'bluebottle', not just for its colour, but also because it is commonly pollinated by flies. Once a serious threat to cereal crops, its decline began in the 1920s with improved methods of seed cleaning. The corncockle suffered similarly. Their defeat came in the 1950s with the widespread use of herbicides. These lovely plants are, however, becoming popular in cottage and 'wildflower' gardens and their seeds are available commercially.

12.75 x 16cm (5 x 6½in)

FIG 5 ▶

A simple landscape and uncomplicated framing features makes a pretty picture. Looking 'through' the buttercups and meadow thistles draws the viewer into the picture and suggests information about the atmosphere and specifics of the location. See also Plate 8.

▲ *FIG 6*

Poppy petals are tissue-paper thin, with a sheen which catches the sunlight to create the impression of a butterfly's shimmering red wing. One of the easiest flowers to sketch, begin by roughing out the shape of the inner petals, then surround them by the outer. In situ the pepper pot at the centre of the flower is often so smothered in pollen that it may be difficult to see it in detail. The pollen is very fine and will blow away with a sharp puff of breath allowing you to complete your sketch.

farmer who tilled nearby fields a century ago had serious problems with the purity of his crops. Similarly, the buttercup (*Ranunculus repens*) in Plate 8 might be a relic of grazing pasture disastrously overtaken by its tenacious ancestors. This could prove an almost crippling blow to pre-war dairy farmers as the cattle, refusing to eat the weed, overgrazed the surrounding grass, so allowing the buttercup to spread even more. It could not be removed by hand due to the sheer scale of the task – and ploughing in simply resulted in cutting the creeping runners and creating thousands of potential new plants.

Not all 'weeds' were considered pests. The thistles in both Plates 8 and 9 indicate a landscape rich in butterfly and bird-life. The long-tongued proboscis of butterflies can reach into the narrowest of thistle florets, whilst thistle seed heads attract finches and other small birds. Plants which shield insects such as ladybirds also provide a service to the main field crop – ladybirds feed on aphids and other pests which can decimate vegetable crops. Other nectar-sipping insects aid pollination and small birds draw larger species to an area – owls and kestrels in turn check the population of mice and rats which can plague grain stores and damage haystacks. The loss of such 'weeds' is a mixed blessing.

Larger bloomed species tend toward simple, open-petalled forms – like sunbathers they expose themselves to the warm, summer sky and invite close scrutiny from their admirers. They are perfect models and their attractive simplicity makes the task of analysis a pleasure. Two of these, the field poppy and common mallow (*Malva sylvestris*), are the subjects of our first Masterclass.

The common or field poppy, shown in Fig 6, has a variable amount of black at the centre of each petal, sometimes a broad band, or none at all. The Flanders poppy grown in memory of the fallen from the First World War sports the most black of all, cross-pollinated commercially to emphasise the petal pattern. Traditionally it is said that red and black poppies also sprang from the blood of the soldiers killed at Waterloo. The two inner petals are smaller than the surrounding outer petals so that seen full-faced, two whole petals and two part petals are visible, most apparent when the flower is young and the petals slightly cupped (top). As it becomes older the flower opens fully (centre and as shown in the Masterclass project) and finally fall to leave the pepper-pot seed capsule alone at the top of the stem. Viewed from above, the 'pot' looks like a little wheel, with spokes radiating from its centre.

Open to the sun, the flower casts a shadow – not only on any surrounding subjects, but also on itself: the edges of each element of its design are partly in light and partly in shade. To recreate the reality of the flower we must imagine it in a microcosm of its own, and, deciding where the light originates in our own design, 'shadow line' in stem stitch the elements away from the light

▼ *PLATE 8*

Part of a larger landscape, this delightful Scottish farmhouse nestles in a valley where flowers of cattle grazing pastures surround the home. Apart from being main features of a picture, flowers provide an important device in the shape of framing features (see Plate 6) telling the viewer something of the nature of the more distant landscape. Thistles, buttercups and clover in an encompassing swathe suggest the quality of the distant grassland. Flowers are a real help in making your embroidery work on several levels. Detail shown 28 x 21.5cm (11 x 8½in)

▲ *FIG 7*

The common mallow (Malva sylvestris)*, so
widespread on headlands and dusty verges, is
actually a spectacular flower, almost rivalling its
more aristocratic cousins, the stately hollyhock
and exotic hibiscus. Its strong, even petals are
supported by tough, short sepals only just visible
behind the open flower. A heliotrope pink base
colour is shot through with darker veins. At the
core of each flower is a bunch of pollen-bearing
stamens, very attractive to bees which often
emerge from the flowers dusted a dusky pink.*

source. Then, to capture the structure of the flower, we must reflect its simplicity by the use of an elementary technique, *opus plumarium*, or 'feather work'. Feather work is so called because it imitates the way in which a bird's feathers lie on its body: smoothly and yet with an infinite capacity to change direction. The angle of the stitches sweeps around without breaking the flow of the stitching itself and this in turn catches the light, refracting it back from the stitching, giving the impression of three-dimensional reality. Creating an impression of light and shade within the design by the use of shadow lining, and using 'real' light to catch the flow of the stitches themselves we can begin to describe the flower itself. Descriptions of these techniques are to be found in Stitch Variations (page 92).

The open-faced common mallow has much in common with the poppy: it is symmetrical and the stitches creating each pink petal fall back to a single 'core'. The stamens form a tall, coned pyramid, emphasised by a tracery of deeper pink, guiding insects toward its nectar and pollen (Fig 7). Seed and shooting stitches respectively create these features: both simple, straight stitches. The strong, broad leaves are worked in *opus plumarium* angled toward an elongated core, formed by a central vein of stem stitching.

As early as the eighth century BC, young leaves and shoots of the common mallow were used as a vegetable. In England it was part of the Roman army's diet during their occupation. In medieval times it was considered a sovereign remedy against the 'over lustful heart', promoting calm and serenity in the breast of the most desperate jilted lover. The same lover might have discovered his sweetheart's infidelity by asking the poppy. Folklore asserts that a poppy petal placed in the open palm and struck with the fist will produce a sharp snapping sound if your lover is faithful. If the blow results in silence . . .

I find that knowing something of the history and folk traditions relating to a subject adds immeasurably to the pleasure of its interpretation. We have also discussed the structure and habitat of our Masterclass subjects. Now, by the use of five easy techniques: shadow lining in stem and straight stitch, *opus plumarium*, seed and shooting stitch, we can begin to enjoy the actual embroidery of simple flowers and foliage.

◀ *PLATE 9*

A floral study need not be solely flowers: a plant's life cycle stages can overlap, with buds, seed heads and fruit appearing in a single picture.

St John's wort (Hypericum perforatum) is a common plant of arable headlands. The yellow-orange pompons at the centre of each flower give way to three-celled seed capsules, surrounded by the withered remains of the flower – a rather spiky shape echoed by the meadow thistle (Cirsium dissectum). The colour of the seed heads echoes the fruits of the tutsan (Hypericum androsaemum) and so all main features are drawn together.

10.75 x 16cm (4¼ x 6½in)

POPPIES AND MALLOW

Our first Masterclass features two of the most striking flowers of field and pasture,

the field poppy and common mallow. Both flowers have simple 'open' faces, complemented

by round buds and, in the case of the mallow, broad, simple leaves.

Work this design on a pale fabric (see Materials, page 88). Transfer the design as laid out in the template on page 18, making sure that all the details are transferred onto your fabric, and mount your design into a tambour hoop (see Basic Techniques, pages 90–91).

TECHNIQUES

Only five basic stitches are required to create this picture:

Stem stitch • Straight stitch • *Opus plumarium*
Seed stitch • Shooting stitch

Refer to Stitch Variations (page 92) if you are unsure of their exact application and then work your way, sequence by sequence, through the detailed instructions for this Masterclass. It is best to work one element of the design at a time; for example finish all the poppies before moving on to the mallow flowers and foliage. In this way you will develop a 'rhythm' to your stitching, becoming familiar with one technique before moving on to the next. If you are right handed, position the screw mechanism of your tambour hoop to the top left of the design; if left handed, to the top right. This will lessen the chance of your thread catching in the screw as you work. Relax and enjoy your embroidery!

PLATE 10 ▶

Masterclass One: Embroidery shown life size 19 x 19cm (7½ x 7½ in)

Carefully transfer the design onto your background material using the template shown (see Basic Techniques, page 90). Make sure that you have included all of the details featured before you begin stitching.

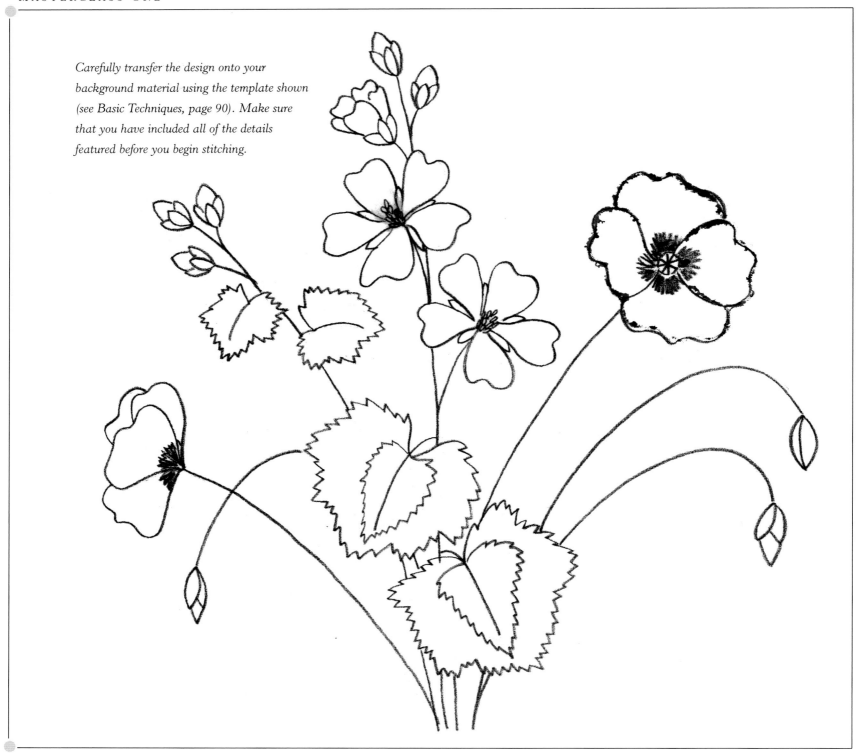

SUGGESTED COLOURS

0 Black

1 Bright red

2 Yellow green

3 Dark green

4 Pale green

5 Mauve

6 Pink

7 Dusky pink

8 Deep pink

Using the colour chart as a guide, choose your threads and colours according to the advice given in the Introduction (page 7). Remember that the shades suggested in the colour chart can be varied to suit your own tastes, but be methodical in the application of your chosen colours, keeping, for instance, all the stems of the poppy a similar colour, and the upper and lower sepals of the mallow buds and flowers to a pre-determined range of shades. Identification of the shade numbers by names (see right) should help with this process. Don't be afraid to follow your own creative impulses in the choice of thread texture and colourway – this is what makes the finished picture unique to you.

DESIGN NOTES

In this study, the imagined light source within the picture comes from almost immediately above

the subject and slightly to the right. Put a pin in your fabric with the tip pointing in this

direction as a reference point. In black (0), shadow line every part of the design on the underside of

each element, referring to the main photograph of the embroidery on page 17 and to the

detailed close-ups that follow. You need not complete all the shadow lining in one operation, but

always make sure it is in situ *before you begin the filling stitches on any individual section.*

BEGIN WITH THE POPPIES...

If you have a variety of thread gauges at your disposal, use a slightly finer
gauge for the poppy petals which, in nature, are tissue-paper thin.
Remember that although in the photograph of the embroidered poppy,
there appears to be several shades of red used, this is an illusion created
by the sweep of the stitches reflecting light. In fact only one shade
of red is used!

1 After shadow lining, work the first strata of radial *opus plumarium* in black (0)
close to the centre of the large flower. Work the two smaller petals first, followed
by the larger. When this strata is complete work a second broad strata of stitching in
bright red (1) to complete the smaller petals. Work each petal from a middle point,
fanning the stitches out toward the outer edges, as shown on the lower petal.
Where the *opus plumarium* meets the shadow line, closely abut the filling stitches
to the shadow line – do not stitch through it, but do not allow a void to show.

2 Complete the stitching of the outer strata of the petals. Where the large upper petal abuts the smaller inner petals (without a shadow line intervening) leave a void between the two elements.

In yellow green (2) work a narrow strata of radial *opus plumarium* at the centre of the flower, slipping the stitches into the 'wheel' creating the pepper pot. Allow your stitches to merge with the shadow line to create a naturalistic effect.

Work the stem of the flower in fine stem stitch in yellow green, the stitches closely abutting the shadow line.

3 Work the rest of the poppy stems in similar style, and complete both the inner and outer strata of *opus plumarium* on the second poppy head. In the detail (left) we see the flower in profile, but the sweep of the stitches is effected in the same manner as above.

Work the poppy bud in three sections. Respectively, create two lozenges of *opus plumarium* in yellow green and dark green (3), followed by a half lozenge in bright red.

4 Repeat the sequence of stitching to create the lower bud. For the upper bud, work a lozenge in yellow green and sweep an arc of directional *opus plumarium* to its left in dark green.

MOVING ON TO THE MALLOWS...

After completing your shadow lining, begin by working the mallow stems in dark green in a slightly broader stem stitch than that used for the poppies. Remember, the transferred design cannot convey anything of the 'character' of the plant – this comes with your embroidery. Emphasise the strong, upright nature of the mallow's stems by taking bold, vigorous stitches to create these lines; similarly, work the veins at the centre of the leaves.

6 Work the upper buds as already described. For the sepals of the half open flower, follow the same principles as the bud sepals; then fill in each section of petal in radial *opus plumarium*, the three closest in mauve, the two part-petals showing behind in pink (6).

5 Work the buds' sepals in three lozenges of *opus plumarium* in dark green and pale green (4) respectively and the petals of the buds in a single stratum of mauve (5).

Create the small leaves by working broad arcs of directional *opus plumarium*: first the upper sides as shown in the left-hand leaf, and then the lower, allowing the stitches to abut the central veins. Where the shadow line is represented by a single straight stitch (such as on the

underside of the upper edge leaf serrations) make sure that the angle of your filling stitches allows you to both fill the serration and abut the shadow line.

7 Work the pollen mass at the centre of each flower in seed stitch in dusty pink (7). Angle your seed stitches so that they flow uniformly. Work the sepals behind the petals in lozenges, or part lozenges, of pale green and dark green. Each petal should be embroidered in a single broad strata of radial *opus plumarium*, beginning at a middle point and fanning out toward the edges. Leave a narrow void between the fields of the petals and the seed stitches creating the pollen masses. The dark veins in each petal should be worked in shooting stitch in deep pink (8). Carefully angling the stitches outward from the centre of each flower, use as many as necessary to create the desired effect. The number of stitches needed will depend upon the gauge of your chosen thread: the finer your thread, the more you will be able to work without crowding the stitches at the centre of the flower – in any case use no more than five or six to maintain a delicate tracery.

8 The large leaves are worked in two strata of directional *opus plumarium* in pale green and dark green. Work the inner strata first, creating the arc by sweeping the angle of stitches smoothly around and abutting the central vein. Work the outer strata at an angle to match the inner, feeding the stitches smoothly together, as shown on the upper leaf. Always work from the apex of the leaf inward. On the topmost of the two leaves shown here, the second strata of stitches on the lower side of the leaf progress from the tip of the leaf toward its base; the second strata of the upper side has not yet been worked; while the lower leaf is complete.

CHAPTER TWO

THE COTTAGE GARDEN

In the cool of the evening, after the heat of a sunny summer afternoon, the cottage garden is a

magical place of dappled twilight and silken shadows amid still vibrant colours. It is a subtle patchwork

of flower beds and borders, often rich with the delicious scent of night-opening blooms.

Probably the easiest place to become familiar with a variety of different types of flowers is in our own gardens, and the traditional 'country garden', is blessed with an inspirational mix of cultivated species and wildflowers, climbing shrubs and rambling roses. Annuals and biennials reach maturity, seed themselves and spring into fresh life as seedlings, whilst perennials flourish year after year and the herbaceous border becomes a mass of diverse shapes and shades. Away from the garden itself, flower arranging and embroidery have much in common when it comes to choosing and combining the right elements to create a pleasing whole.

Whilst there is always a place for artistic license in assembling a design, it is still important to know the basic growth habits of your subjects. Although Plate 11 shows a stylised arrangement of garden flowers, positioned to form a roundel, the basic characteristic growth patterns of each species has been retained. The polyanthus is low growing and so acts as an anchor for the whole, the stately foxgloves curve elegantly above the shrub rose and so on. The scrambling habit of the nasturtiums is suggested by its position at the top of the circle, whilst to the left the mock orange and tobacco plants are kept slightly apart as they are both highly perfumed. Plate 11 also shows how many 'old-fashioned' varieties of plants are available in a wide range of colours; packets of annual seeds are 'mixed' and self-seeded biennials (such as foxgloves) cross-pollinate to create new shades.

◀ *PLATE 11*

Against a black background, the vibrant colours of a cottage border make a spectacular design and an embroidery inspired by such a garden should be equally as unpredictable. Each of the intertwined subjects in this study (except the mock orange) may be found in vastly diverse colours. I sketched the design in pencil and only when I began the embroidery itself did I decide which shades to use. From the bottom, clockwise: polyanthus hybrids, rambling roses, foxgloves (Digitalis purpurea), nasturtiums (Tropaeolum), mock orange (Philadelphus coronarius) and tobacco plants (Nicotiana).
23 x 23cm (9 x 9in)

▲ *FIG 8*

*Hollyhocks (*Altcea (Althaea) rosea*) are a very old garden plant – its ancestry can be traced back 500 years to the formal gardens of the Middle Ages. It is believed to have originated in the Mediterranean and spread both west and east (as far as China). Differing from it cousins in the mallow family mainly by virtue of its vigorous habit, its flowers and leaves may be approached in simple radial and directional opus plumarium.*

Cottage garden plants can often be traced back to their first cultivation, taken from the wild for food or medicine. Their names can be even more ancient. Whilst digitalis was first used to treat heart complaints in 1785, it was well known 1,000 years earlier and the Anglo Saxons named it a glove not to enclose fingers, but after a musical instrument with many tiny bells – the 'gliew'.

In early summer my own garden is an old-fashioned mass of foxgloves, geraniums and evening primroses. Containers are filled with different annuals each year – petunias, sweet peas and morning glory are all favourites. Later, fuchsias bring flashes of vibrant colour and throughout the year a special area is left completely wild. There, grasses, nettles and other 'weeds' are allowed to grow tall, mature and seed at will, providing food and breeding places for moths, butterflies and other beneficial insects – and a cool, green haven for my cat during even the hottest midday. To see elephant hawkmoths sipping nectar from willowherbs in your own garden is a thrill never to be forgotten.

Hollyhocks (Fig 8) are cousins of the common mallow, featured in Masterclass One. They share its upright bearing and the essentially open, dinner plate-shaped flower of the field poppy and could be worked using the techniques we have already explored. Their large petals and strong leaves, however, are less likely to be seen full-face as their tightly packed flower spike means that both petals and leaves are often pushed out of shape by their neighbours. Petals are seen reflexing, leaves curving inward, or flexing outward from the stem. To render these successfully we must begin to elaborate the sweep of our stitches into new directions. This technique is known as 'opposite angle embroidery'.

Plate 12 shows sweet peas clambering up a dusty red-brick wall. Not only are these plants highly attractive *in situ*, they are marvellous for cutting and the older varieties retain the glorious heady perfume of the original specimens brought to England from Sicily in 1699. Although there are newer dwarf varieties which need little or no support, I still love to see blooms scrambling up old walls, over low sheds and into hedges amid a hastily assembled rigging of string and bamboo canes.

◄ *PLATE 12*

Sweet peas (Lathyrus odoratus) *are one of the staples of any country garden. Here, a warm red brick wall is suggested by closely massed seed stitches worked randomly and almost completely obscuring the background fabric. The flowers and leaves are worked in shiny sleave silk and the wall in stranded cotton to create the contrasting matt effect necessary to suggest its rough, weather-beaten texture. The stems of the sweet pea, as they thicken toward their base, are excellent examples of graduated stem stitch.*

10 x 14cm (4 x 5½in)

PLATE 13 ▶

Its variety of colours makes the anemone a perfect subject for a study of a single species, as monotony of shading may be avoided. Like herb Robert (see Masterclass Two page 39) the mature leaves of the anemone tend to become reddish as they age, which adds more interest to the study. Using a device such as the flying petals to add movement to the design is a careful balancing act – too many and they will swamp the picture, too few and they will be disjointed. By including two petals on the ground, a further dimension is added.

9.5 x 9.5cm (3¾ x 3¾in)

The poke-bonnet shapes of the flowers, all seen in profile, are worked in sweeping arcs of radial *opus plumarium* and supported by coiling stems and tendrils in fine and graduating stem stitch. The large leaf to the right comprises two opposing areas of directional *opus plumarium*, but the lower leaf shows an area of its underside. This up-turned curve must be worked at an angle exactly opposite to the adjacent stitching to create the impression of its differing behaviour. This is an essential concept which will arise throughout flower portraiture. In Masterclass Two we will begin its interpretation.

In a simple study, such as Plate 13, opposite angle embroidery gives curve and movement to the flying petals of the windflower (*Anenome blanda*). This spring flower, as its country name suggests, blooms amid the March winds. The generic name of this species comes from the Greek word *anemos*, meaning wind, because the petals are so easily shed in the breeze. It is rare to see the natural world either static or 'full frontal'. To capture its mobile, three-dimensional character we must think laterally, abandon the idea of 'still life', and use stitch variations which allow us scope to build up layers of perspective.

A single fuchsia flower, with buds and leaves and a hovering bumble bee is enough to create a delightful miniature (Plate 14). In a simple frame, this microcosm of the cottage garden still speaks volumes. The cultivar 'Party Frock' has exquisite dancing heads of pink and blue, the lower petals shot through with deeper pink (use shooting stitch, as explained in Masterclass One), its long, delicate style and stamens tipped with pollen-covered stigma and anthers. Bees become prettily dusted as they brush beneath each bloom. The transparent wing of the bumble bee is worked over the stamens, allowing them to be seen through the gauzy effect of the fine straight stitching. This simple three-dimensional trick gives depth and reality to the subject. Elements of a design which are suspended between a background feature and the viewer (the bee's wing) or stand proud, such as the pollen-bearing organs of many flowers, often need to be worked over the underlying embroidery. This stitching must be worked freehand, but need not be as daunting as it first appears.

The evening primroses (*Oenothera missourienses*) in Masterclass Two have leaves and petals which curve and flex, and pollen masses which need careful interpretation. Some evening primroses, true to their name, open only at night. Many, however, are day blooming and these are known, enchantingly, as 'sundrops'. I have chosen Sundrop Ozark, one of the smaller species, an imported English garden favourite, native to the USA. Its reddish-beige stems contrast prettily with the pale silver yellow of its petals; its leaves are simple, slim and sharply elliptic. At the centre of each flower the style and stamens stand proud, the anthers in the shape of narrow sickle moons (see Fig 11). They

▼ *PLATE 14*

A variety of presentation and framing styles adds scope to your choice of initial design. A tiny study such as this might be dwarfed by a traditional frame, and a delicate fob-topped silver frame is ideal. The two small leaves are given a three-dimensional quality by the use of opposite angle stitching (see text and Masterclass Two page 36) which is particularly effective on a small subject. The left-hand leaf, in particular, seems to spring forward toward the viewer.

7.5cm (3in) square including frame

▲ *FIG 9*

Within the family Geraniaceae, *'geraniums', the* Pelargonium *is often referred to, wrongly, as the 'cottage geranium', so beloved of window-sills, front porches and greenhouses. It is, in fact, a separate genus and does not share any of the crane's-bills' characteristics. Like the* polyanthus *in Plate 11 (page 24), the simple, open-faced flowers massed together create an effective bank of colour which can be built up to cover a broad field of fabric. The leaves are very attractive, and would be worked in several strata of radial* opus plumarium.

are in shades of yellow and pale green and must be emphasised by their own fine shadow lining. This process is explained in detail in Masterclass Two. As an alternative to this very fine over-stitching, tiny bugle and seed beads can be substituted to create a slightly more stylised effect. Whilst the former interpretation is shown in the completed Masterclass study in Plate 15, the latter is shown and explained in step 5 on page 38.

The composition of a successful flower design – in common with flower arrangement – lies in a subtle blend of complementary and contrasting elements. For our Masterclass, the large, flashy blooms of the evening primrose share the limelight with the delicate, pastel pink flowers of herb Robert (*Geranium robertium*) and their slim leaves are juxtaposed with the deeply toothed, compound leaves so typical of the geranium family (see also Fig 9). The pinkish colours of the stems are common to both plants, in the case of herb Robert, deepening to red on the more mature leaves. Together the subjects make an attractive combination, the flow of the sinuous stems leading the eye from one element to the next.

The geranium (or crane's-bill) family is large and diverse. In the flower border these hardy perennial plants spread quickly and if not cut back each year can grow to ungainly proportions. However, as ground cover I find them welcome, smothering unwanted weeds and, in a cottage garden setting, their vigorous growth is less overwhelming. Cultivated varieties are surprisingly similar to their wild cousins (though with larger blooms), but herb Robert is still classed officially as a wildflower. It was probably first grown in a garden setting in the Middle Ages, when according to the 'doctrine of signatures' (a theory which held that plants that looked like a certain part of the human body would be beneficial to that part), it was used to treat blood disorders because of its red leaves. It has been suggested that 'robert' is a corruption of the Latin *ruber* meaning red, or it may have been named for Robert, a medieval Duke of Normandy the patron of a then well-known medical tract. The Tudors associated it with Robert Dudley, the favourite of Queen Elizabeth I – her 'Sweet Robin'.

Essentially, the herb Robert's small flowers are worked similarly to those of the larger plant, the radial *opus plumarium* falling back to the central core of each bloom, but special care should be taken on delicate subjects to position the stitches as accurately as possible. The deeply indented leaves present a greater challenge, but the principle of the stitching is the same as for a simple ovate form. The central vein of each leaf should first be worked in stem stitch and the directional *opus plumarium* worked towards it, slipping down toward the base, the length of the stitches varying in accordance with the distance between the outline of the leaf and the central vein. This will be explored in detail in the Masterclass.

One key to successful flower portraiture is reality (see Plate 13, page 28). To suggest an actual location and point of growth for our subjects gives an added sense of that reality, easily achieved by including the impression of low-growing grasses at the foot of the study. These can be as simple as a few long straight stitches, in one or more shades, angled slightly toward their base. They should flow in and around the main subjects, and worked freehand after completion of the rest of the design. The spontaneity of working a few stitches as and where you feel they would be most effective not only gives a lively and realistic fillip to the study, but also is a fun way to finish a project!

▲ *FIG 10*

The flowers of the tobacco plant, although brightly coloured in shades from cream through yellow and green to bright red, are fairly insignificant compared to their breathtaking perfume which is released at dusk. Similarly, night-scented stocks (Matthiola bicornis) are poor relations to their showy cousins the summer stocks – but their scent is unforgettable. Shown here in pink, they are, however, delicate and sinuous and in embroidery design can be used to good effect. I created an atmospheric night scene featuring their gentle, curving fronds in my recent book The Myth and Magic of Embroidery.

FIG 11 ▶

The structure of the evening primrose itself is simple but the style and stigma arrangement needs careful analysis. To work them accurately, spread the stamens out (some may appear to flex forward toward the viewer) through a 360 degree arc. This will give you more room to work the anthers individually. The style and stigma should be worked last; this feature is longer than the stamens and should extend beyond the tips of the anthers. The working is explained in detail in Masterclass Two, page 38.

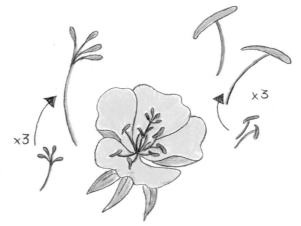

EVENING PRIMROSES AND HERB ROBERT

The subjects in our second Masterclass are two plants which both contrast and complement each other. The evening primroses are bold and sinuous, whilst the herb Robert presents a delicate tracery of irregular outlines. Pink, beige and orange-red tones in the leaves and sepals draw the two together and create a harmony of shades both in the foliage and stems.

This design should be worked on a pale fabric (see Materials, page 88). Trace and transfer the outline from the template on page 34 (see Basic Techniques, page 90). You will see that fine details, such as the styles and stigmas of the evening primroses and the 'whiskers' on the herb Robert buds are omitted from the template. These will be added freehand. Centralise and mount your fabric into a tambour hoop (see page 91).

Refresh your memory by referring to Stitch Variations (page 92) if necessary and then work your way through the Masterclass. Remember to keep your fabric as taut as possible within the tambour hoop. This will make your stitches lie smoothly and will help when over-stitching the details at the centre of the evening primroses.

TECHNIQUES

We have used all these techniques before, with the exception of opposite angle stitching, a variation on opus plumarium:

Stem stitch • Straight stitch • *Opus plumarium*
Seed stitch • Opposite angle stitching

PLATE 15 ▶

Masterclass Two: Embroidery shown life size 21.5 x 21cm (8½ x 8¼in)

*Carefully transfer the design onto your
background material using the template
shown (see Basic Techniques, page 90).
Make sure that you have included
all of the details featured before
you begin stitching.*

SUGGESTED COLOURS

1 Black
2 Pink/beige
3 Olive green
4 Very pale green
5 Leaf green
6 Pale beige
7 Orange
8 Bright green
9 Yellow
10 Red/orange
11 Yellow green
12 Mauve/pink

Refer to the colour chart and choose your colours. As before, these can vary slightly according to your tastes, but keep to the basic format of name/number so that you will apply the correct sequence of colours. As our Masterclass projects become more complex, the colour charts will portray a greater range of shades. Very small fields of colour may not be annotated – use your judgement as to which shades to use. For instance, if a type of leaf is portrayed in shades 3 and 4 on upper and lower sides throughout the rest of the chart, follow this format throughout.

DESIGN NOTES

The imagined light source in this study comes from immediately above the subject. Referring to Plate 15, the completed Masterclass study, and to the various close-up studies that follow, work the shadow line in black (1) on the underside of each element. On the sinuous elements use a fine stem stitch and on irregular shapes, such as the leaves of the herb Robert, use fragmented shadow lining (see Stitch Variations, page 92). Do not agonise too much over your shadow lining — it need not exactly follow the example of the details shown — remember that it is designed only to suggest the light source, not set it in stone.

BEGIN WITH THE EVENING PRIMROSES...

Work the main stems in graduated stem stitch in pink/beige (2), the flower stalks in narrow stem stitch in olive green (3) and the leaf veins and petioles (stalks) in narrow stem stitch in very pale green (4).

1 Work the upper sides of each evening primrose leaf in directional *opus plumarium* in olive green and the lower in leaf green (5). (For the moment do not work the herb Robert leaf shown.) The large leaves at the base of the stem are curving upward, presenting an area of their undersides to the viewer. In very pale green, work these fields in opposite angle stitching. The correct angle can always be calculated by estimating the angle of the stitches which would be used should the element of the design *not* be flexed or curving. Once this been calculated according to the usual rules of *opus plumarium*, the exactly opposite angle of stitching should be used on the appropriate field. Work the half open bud sepals (top) in lozenges and half lozenges of radial *opus plumarium* in very pale green, pale beige (6) and pink/beige respectively and the petal buds in yellow (9).

2 Work each petal of the open evening primrose flower in a single long stratum of radial *opus plumarium* in yellow, the upper and middle sepals in arcs of directional *opus plumarium* in very pale green and olive green respectively and the lower sepal in radial *opus plumarium* in leaf green.

The bursting buds (top and left) should be stitched in the same sequence as the buds in step 1, with the bud petals in broader sweeps of yellow.

3 This flower is seen at a slight angle – the lower petal flops forward toward the viewer (the angle of the stitching continues to follow the format of normal radial *opus plumarium*, as we are seeing the upper surface of the petal). To the right and left of the flower the petal edges curl inwards and opposite angle stitching must be used to capture this effect. Slip your stitches smoothly down into the throat of the flower creating a three-dimensional effect by the angle of the stitching. This stitching is shown completed in the detail of step 5.

Work the sepals in three arcs of directional *opus plumarium* in (left to right) leaf green, olive green and very pale green.

The immature buds (right) show only a tiny area of yellow at the tip of the lower bud. Work the sepals in lozenges of radial *opus plumarium* in pale beige (a small inner strata of pink/beige at the base of the upper bud gives depth to the feature) and narrow sweeps of very pale green.

4 The pollen masses at the centre of the evening primroses may be approached in two ways: choose whichever appeals to you! A strictly botanical study of the style, stigma and stamens is achieved by the use of shadow lining, stem and straight stitches. Stitching over the top of the underlying radial *opus plumarium*, work shadow lining in black to suggest the positions of the fine details, as shown by the four outlines for anthers in the bottom right quadrant (refer to colour chart and completed Masterclass study for positioning). Immediately abutting the fine shadow lines work stem and straight stitch in orange (7) to create the stamens and anthers, and in bright green (8) for the style and stigma. Leave your stitching fairly loose, to avoid pulling the underlying stitches out of position.

5 Alternatively, the pollen masses may be represented in a more stylised way by using, for each flower, eight short bugle beads in a gold/orange shade to suggest the anthers and a cluster of four small seed beads in bright green for the stigma. Attach the beads loosely, with a fine, self-coloured thread.

MOVING ON TO THE HERB ROBERT...

Work the main stems and flower stalks in narrow stem stitch in olive green and the petioles and leaf veins in red/orange (10). The stipules and bracts are small lozenges of radial *opus plumarium* in red/orange.

6 Referring to the colour chart, in yellow green (11), leaf green and red/orange, work the upper and lower sides of each leaf in directional *opus plumarium*. Following the principles of directional stitching, sweep your stitches inwards toward the elongated growing points created by the central veins, varying the lengths of your stitches as necessary to follow the outline of the outer edge of the leaf. Work the upper and central clusters of leaves (see Plate 15) similarly.

7 The lower flower shows the fragmented shadow lining necessary for a small, irregular motif such as the herb Robert. Work each petal in mauve/pink (12) in a single short strata of radial *opus plumarium* (centre) and suggest the sepals and centre of each by seed stitches in leaf green (top). I have worked the petals in very fine silk, mixing strands of mauve and pink together in the needle to give a slightly striated effect. If your chosen thread is too thick the achieve this effect, choose a colour somewhere between the two.

Work the buds in chubby lozenges of radial *opus plumarium* in olive green and add a few whiskers at the tip of each – simple straight stitches, slightly angled, in red/orange.

Finally, work a few long, straight stitches at the intersection of all the stems at the base of the motif. Choose a green which complements your other shades, and, if you are working principally in silk, try a contrasting texture such as stranded cotton to give a subtle variation of effect. Don't be afraid to stitch over underlying features – this adds a sense of reality.

HELEN M.
STEVENS

CHAPTER THREE

WAYSIDES

Since mankind first established settlements and began regularly to journey between them, tracks,

paths and roadways have woven their way through the countryside. As agriculture became

established, field systems were divided by hedgerows, sometimes running alongside the lanes, and

together created a softly padded quilt of meandering boundaries and highways.

Both hedges and waysides are important habitats offering a wide variety of micro-climates to the flora and fauna which make homes in their shrubs or grasses. As an ancient hedge snakes through fields and meadows, parts catch all available sunlight whilst other areas are in perpetual shadow. Depending upon the make-up of the hedge, the surrounding soil may be dry or moist and underlying geological features may be traversed, changing the chemistry of the soil. Roadside verges, too, change their nature as the miles pass. The same greensward may extend from valley to hill top, may run alongside dry stone walling or layered hawthorn, or form an unbroken stretch from county lane, to busy road and finally motorway.

The interwoven plants of the wayside and hedgerow seem particularly appropriate subjects for embroidery – silky leaves, sinuous, coiling stems, sharply contrasting shapes all lend a new dimension to design and offer the embroiderer inspiration and challenge (see Fig 12). And they are not difficult to find – a drive in the countryside, a picnic in a rural setting, taking note of the plants thriving on the verges of the motorway can suggest new projects. The sheer variety of size, shape and colour can be daunting, but their diversity offers some fascinating combinations.

◀ *PLATE 16*

The impressionistic suggestion of wildflowers along this roadside echoes the colours used in the framing features of the picture, and serves to draw the viewer into the scene. From the extreme left, clockwise are: great mullein, bindweed, hedge bindweed, meadow cranesbill, silverweed and ribwort plantain.

Don't be tempted to 'overwork' a small landscape such as this – as in water-colour painting, spontaneity should be your watchword. Similarly, the sky is simply indicated by just two blue swathes. See also the comments with regard to the design of this chapter's Masterclass project.

25.5 x 23.5cm (10 x 9¼in)

▲ *FIG 12*

*Climbing plants of the hedgerow share many design characteristics: black bryony (*Tamus communis) *and hops (*Humulus lupulus) *both climb by twining around their hosts and can create long leafy ropes, thickening toward their base. Always work in graduating stem stitch to capture an authentic effect. Broad, sweeping arcs of directional* opus plumarium, *together with opposite angle stitching would be used on the leaves, and the scales of the hops shadow lined individually (if working on pale fabric) similarly to the seeding head of the plantain.*

Plate 16 was suggested by a country road near my home. Most country roads – even quiet lanes – are now surfaced, but a silver-grey tarmac, dotted with watery blue puddles after a recent shower can be attractive. Here, as the road itself disappears into the landscape, its course can be traced by the distant hedgerow heading the eye to the horizon. One side of the lane is bounded by a tall, well-tended hedge, the other by a fence and the lane winds between agricultural land and summer pasture for horses. Rabbits graze the verges, which are also occasionally mown, and the well-trimmed hedge is nevertheless invaded by great swathes of bindweed, the pink and white 'morning glory' of the English countryside. Insects are abundant, birds nest in the shrubs – both feeding on and amongst the tangle of plants.

The tall, yellow spikes of the great mullein (*Verbascum thapsus*) are a reminder of days before cotton was introduced to Britain – the downy, white coating on the underside of its leaves was gathered to make candlewicks. Mixing two shades of thread in a single needle creates the effect of this soft 'rabbit's-ear' texture, and the technique has been used again on the leaves of the silverweed (*Potentilla anserina*). Both these attractive yellow-flowered plants have simple, five-petalled flowers and centrally veined, roughly elliptical leaves (which we have explored already – see page 36). The pretty, open-faced meadow crane's-bill (*Geranium pratense*) is a close relation of herb Robert (see Masterclass Two) and its deeply serrated leaves should be approached in the same manner. The bindweeds and plantain, however, both present elements which we have not yet interpreted.

Generations of farmers and gardeners have tried unsuccessfully to eliminate bindweeds from their borders. True bindweed (*Convolvulus arvensis*) grows quickly (its tenacious stem can complete a full anti-clockwise circle in under two hours) and it is incredibly strong. Its roots spread horizontally underground and can push up right through a tarmacked road! The larger-flowered hedge bindweed (*Calystegia sepium ssp sepium*) is slightly easier to control. Its roots are shallower but its stem is fibrous, earning it the country name of 'rope-bind'. To emphasise the tough, vigorous properties of the stems they should be worked in graduating stem stitch (see Stitch Variations, page 92), the delicate tendrils giving way to thicker, stronger lines as they reach their base. Leaves are simple, centrally veined, and worked in arcs of directional *opus plumarium*. The trumpet-shaped flowers are formed of a single, fused petal sloping down sharply into a deep throat protecting the nectar secreted at the base of the flower. The complete 360 degree circuit of radial *opus plumarium* takes the technique to its ultimate extent and is fully explored in this chapter's Masterclass.

Plantain (see Fig 13 overleaf) thrives wherever the ground is well trodden. Ancient trackways and Roman roads still reflect the pounding of many feet, as plantains extend along their length. In North America the native peoples called greater plantain 'white man's foot' as it appeared as soon as an immigrant settler crossed their land. The seeds adhere to the sole of shoe or boot and disperse with the traveller. The tough, broad leaves sport several fibrous veins along their length and should be embroidered in arcs of directional *opus plumarium*, each separated by a stem-stitched vein. The flower heads look like seeding bodies, each worked in a series of tiny, shadow-lined lozenges, with seed stitches overlaid to suggest stamens and anthers.

The winter wayside suggests some pretty effects (see Plate 17). Hawthorn hedges sport berries, or haws, late into the winter and the brightly coloured autumn leaves sometimes also survive to create beautiful combinations of shades and shapes. Although the bindweeds die back at the end of the summer, their dead stems often cling onto their supports and can be suggested by arabesques of couched gold thread, whilst the dead heads of cow parsley and other umbellifors make attractive baskets which collect frost and

▼ *PLATE 17*

To capture a magical scene like this, some aide memoire *is useful. A few quick lines in your sketchbook, a scribbled suggestion of snow caught between the ribs of the cow parsley stems, and a quick highlighting of colour will bring the subject to life later. Jot in an arrow to remind you where the light source comes from, and where to place a reflective white stitch on the berries. Experiment with specialist materials too. Here, sequins are held in place by seed beads so that no stitch crosses the sequins to break the shimmering effect.* 10 x 8.75cm (4 x 3½in)

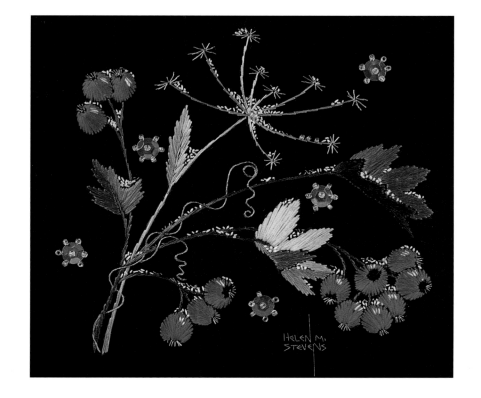

▲ *FIG 13*

The Anglo Saxons called plantains 'warriors' –
the long spear-like seed heads suggested war-like
qualities. The basal rosettes of the greater plantain
(Plantago major) spread horizontally, whilst the
ribwort plantain (Plantago lanceolata) thrusts
upwards (see Plate 16). Carefully angled
directional opus plumarium *between stem*
stitched veins will capture them both.

early snowfalls like magic, up-turned umbrellas. Add a stylised sparkle by stitching translucent sequins and seed beads amongst the foliage to suggest soft, fluffy snowflakes. Working on a black background throws bright colours into very effective relief and allows relatively few shades to create a dramatic impression. Masterclass Three captures the summer wayside in similar, though slightly simpler, forms.

Following a colour theme through subject, thread and background fabric can make a small study highly evocative. Common restharrow (*Ononis repens*) bears a pea-like flower in one of nature's truest pinks (Plate 18). Together with its pale, silvery green foliage it is a delightful 'find' on the roadside, often suggesting that adjacent fields were once tilled by horse-drawn plough. The tough, matted stems and deep roots literally 'stopped the plough', hence its common name. Chopped up by hand and thrown over the hedge onto the roadside, it simply re-rooted and now enjoys many rough grassy headlands, especially on chalky soils. Here, the pink flowers have been emphasised by working the design on a pastel pink fabric, complementing the pinky-beige of the moth and the mauve anthers of the Timothy grass. Cowslips (*Primula veris*) also now find their prime habitat on the verges of country lanes, where they are less prone to herbicides and the destruction of their root systems (Fig 14).

Close inspection of the wayside reveals a whole new panoply of ideas, every sense playing a part in the exploration. The chirrup of the common field grasshopper leads the ear, rather than the eye, to its perch, often amid scrubby, thistly plants on dry, sunny verges (Plate 19). Many thistles have a sweet, musky odour, very attractive to insects. Butterflies in particular enjoy their nectar, but other insects seem to sense that they are protected by the otherwise inhospitable, sharp leaves and flower heads. In Plate 19, the prickly, thrusting shapes of the spear thistle (*Cirsium valgare*) are all sharply directional – every angle is

◀ *PLATE 18*

The low, trailing stems of the common restharrow are easily lost in long grasses, but it enjoys the same habitat as bindweed – if you find the latter it is worth a search for this shy plant. It is shown here with the Kentish Glory moth (Endromis versicolora).

Whilst the use of a coloured background fabric can be useful to emphasise a colour theme, be careful not to choose a shade which will overwhelm your main subject. Pastels are the safest: try to choose a colour at least one shade lighter than the palest of your embroidery threads.
9.5 x 9.5cm (3¾ x 3¾in)

◀ *FIG 14*

Cowslips, relatives of the polyanthus (shown in Plate 11, page 24), make a delicate motif for embroidery. Like many plants which find their homes amid grasses, the suggestion of random blades in and around the base of the plant adds realism (see Masterclass Two). Sketch these in at drawing board stage – they add body to your design and suggest the finished effect – but do not transfer them.

PLATE 19 ▶

Emphasise the three-dimensional, prickly quality
of this thistle study by overlaying various
details: the leaf-tips and spines criss-cross the
underlying features very effectively. It is useful to
have several gauges of thread at your disposal to
emphasise the contrast between the strong fleshy
properties of the leaves and the very fine, rigid
prickles. Two shades of fine thread have been used
together to suggest a slightly downy effect on the
sepals of the thistle head – this technique has also
been used in Plate 16 (see text page 42).
7.5 x 13cm (3 x 5in)

emphasised. Only in the silky florets at the top of the flower head is there a suggestion of softness. The inward curving leaves partly wing the strong upright stem, and take the principle of opposite angle stitching to its limit, as do the reflexing sepals (these are worked in chevron stitch, see Stitch Variations, page 94). Each is tipped by a spine (a single straight stitch) angled to match exactly the direction of the underlying stitching. The florets are stitched in three shades of silk, each worked separately, and becoming finer toward their extremity. A striking image such as this works well without the interference of added grasses or background features. I have used the same principle in this chapter's Masterclass.

Plate 20 (page 49) shows the elegant flower spikes of rosebay willow herb (*Epilobium angustifolium*), together with bindweed. The shape and form of this study is slightly more stylised than our former Masterclass projects: the flowers of the willowherb are fairly complex and mature along the length of their stem at varying rates (see Fig 15). The bindweed forms an impressive arabesque culminating in two open-trumpeted flowers and the whole design suggests that it is part of the broader canvas of the hedgerow.

By working on a black background we eliminate the need for a shadow line which would further complicate the willowherb flower, and use the technique of voiding to define overlapping elements. Long expanses of the willowherb's straight stem (unlike the sinuous coil of the bindweed), would be ungainly and so must be broken up by allowing buds and flowers to interrupt its length. Careful voiding between each element is essential to achieve sharp definition (see Stitch Variations, page 92). Shooting stitches create the tracery at the centre of each petal, and the pollen-bearing bodies are overlaid in techniques we have already practised.

Rosebay willowherb was grown by the Victorians as a garden ornament and was then considered something of a rarity in the wild. It is one of the few wildflowers which is now more common than in previous centuries and thrives particularly well on land disturbed by building – perhaps this explains why it appears at the edges of widened roads such as newly duelled motorways. Driving by a bank of its elegant swaying fronds certainly brightens a long journey. It propagates in two highly effective and efficient ways: by woody roots which spread horizontally sending up new shoots at frequent intervals, and by wind-born seeds. The fruiting capsules at the base of each flower split when mature, releasing billowing clouds of downy-tipped seeds into the wind which are blown to new habitats.

The design of our Masterclass echoes the breezy slip-stream of the roadside. The movement is toward the right – every element sweeps in the same direction. This allows a particularly effective use of 'real' light as it catches the various directional arcs of the stitches and reflects it. When designing your own pictures, don't be afraid to leave certain areas of your canvas blank. Here, the 'empty' area in the bottom right-hand quadrant of the design serves to emphasise the movement of the rest of the design. Oriental design often leaves vast areas of 'nothingness' within a study to give the actual subject greater importance. Avoid the temptation of making your designs too 'busy'. Often, a good maxim to work by is 'the less, the more'.

▼ FIG 15

Individual rosebay willowherb flowers mature down the length of their stem from immature bud (top), through full bud and open flower, immature and finally fruiting seed head (not included in the Masterclass). The pollen masses have been omitted for clarity. Become familiar with the structures before you begin stitching. When you find a complex flower in the field, it is worth sketching the various stages of its development for later reference. We will look at different seed dispersal systems later, in Chapters Four and Five.

ROSEBAY WILLOWHERB AND BINDWEED

Our third Masterclass is an airy study, full of movement and light. It suggests a three-dimensional quality – especially in the trumpet-shaped flowers of the bindweed whose deep throats slope sharply toward their base, contrasting with the more complex, but open, faces of the willowherb.

The design is worked here on a black background. It could of course, be worked on a pale background, to give a completely different effect. If you decide to do so, *don't* forget that you will need to shadow line! Trace and transfer the design from the template as usual.

Remember, when working on black, to be very careful not to smudge the white or yellow transferred line on the fabric as it is lost more easily than darker shades. Centralise and mount into your tambour.

Refer to Stitch Variations (page 92) if necessary and then work your way through the project, detail by detail. If you have a selection of thread gauges at your disposal, in the appropriate shades, use the finer threads to work delicate details such as the centre of the willowherb and the fine tendrils of the bindweed.

TECHNIQUES

Working on black, we use the same techniques as in our previous Masterclasses, but voiding rather than shadow lining is employed to suggest breaks of contour:

Stem stitch • Straight stitch • *Opus plumarium*
Shooting stitch • Seed stitch • Voiding

PLATE 20 ▶

Masterclass Three: Embroidery shown life size 23 x 21.5cm (9 x 8½in)

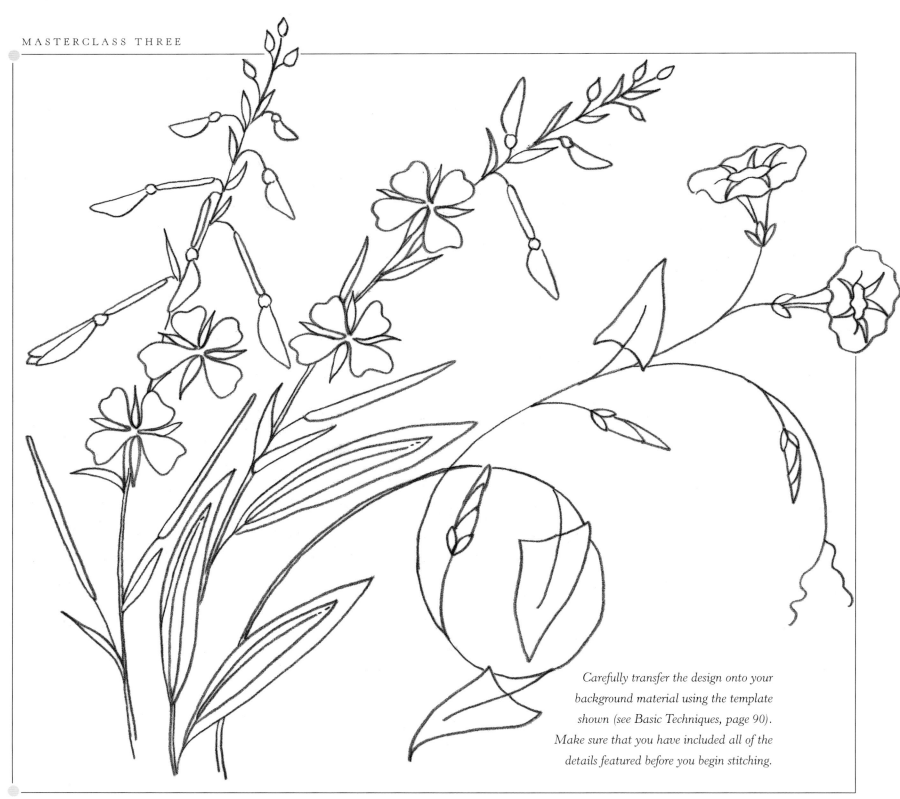

Carefully transfer the design onto your background material using the template shown (see Basic Techniques, page 90). Make sure that you have included all of the details featured before you begin stitching.

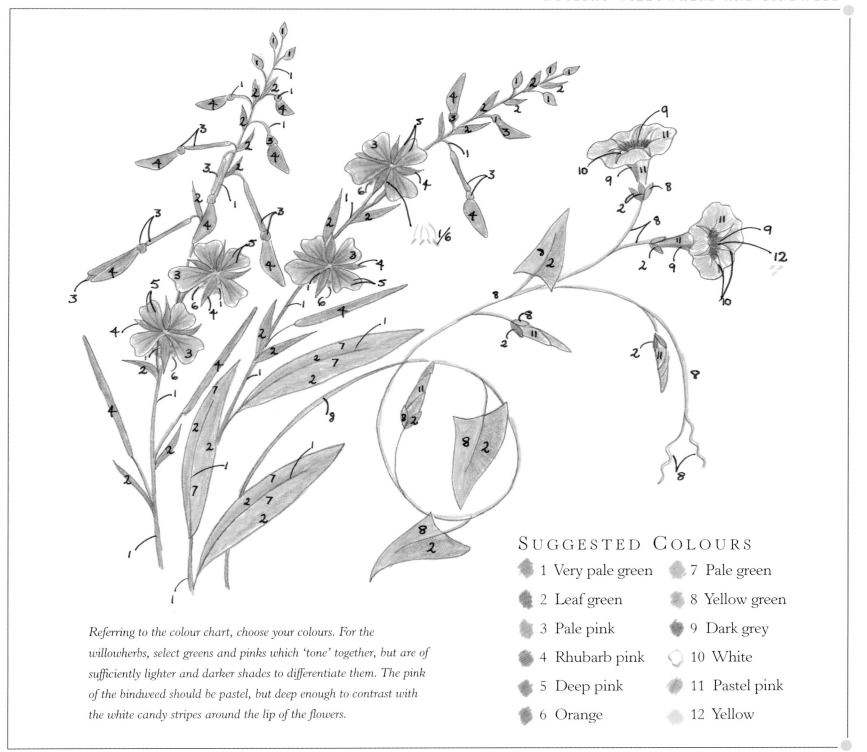

SUGGESTED COLOURS

1 Very pale green   7 Pale green

2 Leaf green   8 Yellow green

3 Pale pink   9 Dark grey

4 Rhubarb pink   10 White

5 Deep pink   11 Pastel pink

6 Orange   12 Yellow

Referring to the colour chart, choose your colours. For the willowherbs, select greens and pinks which 'tone' together, but are of sufficiently lighter and darker shades to differentiate them. The pink of the bindweed should be pastel, but deep enough to contrast with the white candy stripes around the lip of the flowers.

DESIGN NOTES

In a study on a black background, the lack of a shadow line means that the imagined light source within the picture is of secondary importance to the directional sweep of the stitches catching the 'real' light around you. Take particular care with the angle of your stitches. Try to advance it smoothly with no break in the flow of the embroidery.

BEGIN WITH THE ROSEBAY WILLOWHERB...

Work all the stems in graduating stem stitch, and the central veins of the leaves in fine stem stitch in very pale green (1).

1 Work the immature buds in small lozenges of radial *opus plumarium* in very pale green and the bracts at the base of the flower stalks in leaf green (2). Refer to the photograph for the correct directional sweep. At the base of the more mature buds, work broad lozenges in very pale green or pale pink (3) as designated by the colour chart. Void between each section – the width of the void should be approximately equal to the gauge of the thread used. This rule applies throughout the project.

2 The long, immature seed pods at the base of the larger buds should be worked in long radial *opus plumarium* in pale pink, converging only very slightly as they approach the flower stalk. By working shooting stitches in very pale green along their length an effect of integrated pink and green is achieved.

Work the large buds in rhubarb pink (4) radial *opus plumarium*. Take a long straight stitch from

the very tip of the bud to its base, and fan out the *opus plumarium* very slightly toward the top of the bud and more acutely toward its underside. This will emphasise the 'ballet shoe' shape of the bud, so typical of this plant.

3 The opening bud (top left) is worked in two sections of radial *opus plumarium* (as described in step 2) with a tiny half lozenge of pale pink to suggest the emerging flower.

Work the mature flowers feature by feature. Right, the four open petals are worked in radial *opus plumarium*, converging to narrow bases at the centre of the flower. Centre, the sepals are added in long,

narrow lozenges of rhubarb pink, slotting neatly in between the petals. Overlay shooting stitches of deep pink (5) to create the tracery leading to the core. Left, long straight stitches in very pale green (in a fine thread if possible) are worked over the underlying features, to create the stamens, each tipped by a seed stitch in orange (6) for the anthers.

4 The mature seed pods should be worked in very long radial *opus plumarium*, again converging only very slightly toward their base.

The leaves are each worked in four strata of directional *opus plumarium*. Work the inner strata first in pale green (7) and leaf green, allowing the arcs of stitching to fall smoothly toward the central vein of each leaf (top). The outer strata should match the directional stitching of the inner perfectly (centre and bottom).

MOVING ON TO THE BINDWEED...

5 Using a finer gauge of thread (if possible) at the tip, work the stems and tendrils of the bindweed in graduating stem stitch in yellow green (8). Remember always to work *with* the curve of the line to create a smooth, even flow of stitches (see Stitch Variations, page 92). Work the central veins of the leaves in fine stem stitch in yellow green and the leaves themselves in two strata of directional *opus plumarium* in yellow green and leaf green. Sweep the stitches gently at the tip of the leaves and increasingly acutely as they approach their base.

6 Work the bud sepals in small lozenges of radial *opus plumarium* in yellow green and leaf green.

Voiding carefully between each section, work the bud in part lozenges of radial *opus plumarium* in pastel pink (11).

7 Work the flower sepals similarly to those for the buds in step 6.

Top: Work a narrow strata of radial *opus plumarium* in dark grey (9) at the centre of the flower to suggest the deeply shadowed throat of the trumpet and, similarly, a narrow wedge to the left of the trumpet itself.

Bottom: Work sharply triangular arcs of directional *opus plumarium* in white (10), fanning in alternate directions and slipping down towards the 'shadow'.

8 Top: Intersperse radial *opus plumarium* in pastel pink between the narrow white arcs of directional *opus plumarium*, carefully mating the flow of the stitches where they meet. Bottom: Advance the angle of the radial stitching sharply as it rounds the extremities of each flower, and void a line between the base of the grey strata and the stitches creating the nearside of the flower. Allow this void to extend a little between the upper and lower lips of the trumpet.

Continue the 360 degree sweep of the radial work until the circuit is completed and work the lower portion of the trumpet in radial *opus plumarium*, smoothly abutting the grey shadowed area. Tiny seed stitches in yellow (12) to suggest anthers complete each flower.

CHAPTER FOUR

WOODLAND GLADES

A tangled mass of fronds and foliage embroidering the forest floor, dappled sunlight through lush leaves scattering a crazy jigsaw of light and shade, shy flowers, tiny fruits and vibrant splashes of unexpected colour – woodland weaves a magic that is impossible to ignore.

Whilst broad swathes of ancient woodland offer the greatest variety of flora, modern conifer plantations, small copses on heath or common land and even the municipal planting of specially chosen decorative trees and shrubs all provide habitats for flowers which thrive under a protective canopy. Often they are small blooms, too delicate to survive in an open landscape and some are becoming increasingly rare: the bluebells which once carpeted untold acres of English woodland are now, rightly, protected by law, and the location of certain orchids and helleborines, once common, are jealously guarded (see Fig 16).

The leaf litter which strews the woodland floor means that many of the native plants are either strong, tenacious climbers, able to escape the tangle below, or have the ability to spread horizontally, sending delicate but invasive runners or stems through the debris. Both habits suggest delightful design concepts for the embroiderer. The roundel in Plate 21 is composed of ramblers and climbers, together with some vigorous upright species, able to compete with their more unruly neighbours. Added movement is suggested in the design by the holly blue butterfly, a common visitor to woodland glades and fringes, and the intertwining quality of the foliage emphasised by coiling tendrils worked in gold metallic thread. Surface couching, a technique allowing smooth application of threads (such as metallics) too thick to penetrate the fine background fabric, will be fully explored in Chapter Five.

◄ *PLATE 21*

Despite the diversity of subject matter in this woodland roundel, a harmony has been achieved by 'balancing' certain motifs and colours. The dark green leaves top left and bottom right, complex patterning top right and bottom left, yellows both right and left, all serve to lead the eye through and around the design without becoming 'fixed' on any one feature. From the bottom, clockwise are: wild strawberries, early purple orchid, scarlet pimpernel, yellow pimpernel, bittersweet, traveller's joy, ragged robin and yellow archangel.

Embroidery shown life size
22.25 x 22.25cm (8¾ x 8¾in)

▼ *FIG 16*

Although actually orchids, helleborines are usually considered to be significantly different to their cousins to merit separate consideration. They are rather more delicate than most fleshy-stemmed orchids and make a pretty addition to a collection of embroidery designs. If worked on a pale background, particular attention should be paid to shadow lining to define the rather complicated structure of the flowers. From the top, clockwise: red helleborine (Cephalanthera rubra), narrow-leaved helleborine (C. longifolia) and white helleborine (C. damasonium). As suggested by its name, the petals of the latter were once thought to resemble fine linen.

Different seasons offer a variety of subjects. The wild strawberry (*Fragaria vesca*) blooms from April to high summer, its deliciously sweet fruits succeeding the flowers as they mature. Their pretty silver-blue, green foliage thrusts its way through the previous year's dead leaves which render the fruits the same service of protection as the straw covering cultivated strawberries. The scarlet pimpernel (*Anagallis arvensis*) and yellow pimpernel (*Lysimachia nemorum*), both members of the primrose family, share the same scrambling habit, though the scarlet variety prefers a more open location. These sinuous, creeping stems should be worked in fine, reflexing stem stitch (see Stitch Variations, page 92). This more delicate stitch offers a contrast to the broader stem stitch necessary to create the tougher, woody stems of the bittersweet (*Solanum dulcamara*) and the traveller's joy (*Clematis vitalba*).

Climbers, as we have seen in Chapter Three, are a delight for the creative artist in whatever medium they work. For embroiderers in particular, the fluid sweep of stalk and stem leading the eye to flower, fruit or seed, lends both structure and framework to a design. Here, the bittersweet sports not only glossy, deep green leaves, but brilliant blue-purple and yellow flowers and distinctive shiny berries, all at the same time. The traveller's joy, relative of our garden varieties of clematis, has petal-less, long-stamened, creamy flowers which give way to plumed, feathery seed heads (see Fig 17). This abundance of shape and texture requires a variety of techniques to capture its many effects. Carefully angled directional and radial *opus plumarium* describe the leaves, flowers and berries of the bittersweet; straight and seed stitches render the pompon flowers of the clematis, but a new technique is required for the fluffy seed heads – floating embroidery (see Stitch Variations, page 94).

By taking only tiny stitches at the outer and inner extremities of the seed head, working the thread alternately inward and outward from the core and allowing the thread to lie loosely against the background fabric, the effect of each feathery plume 'floating' above the background fabric is convincingly achieved.

The three remaining subjects in Plate 21 are yellow archangel (*Lamiastrum galeobdolon*), ragged robin (*Lychnis flos-cuculi*) and the early purple orchid (*Orchis mascula*). The first two of this trio (to the right of the study), although apparently complex, are worked in techniques already explored: the leaves are simple and centrally veined, the flowers require variations of radial and directional *opus plumarium* (very finely worked in the case of the ragged robin). Seed, chevron and shooting stitches will describe all the other features. Similarly the orchid flowers should now present no problems, but the leaf of the early purple orchid offers a fresh challenge.

Whilst not very common in temperate climates (it is found more often in tropical or exotic species), occasionally we may meet a plant whose leaves or petals sport fairly large spots or blotches of colour wholly contained within another shade. The texture of the feature remains constant – only the colour changes – and we must be able to describe this variation whist keeping the sweep of stitching seemingly unbroken. Round, dull purple spots appear on the leaves of the early purple orchid. To work these effectively, the angle of the main body of the leaf should be carefully calculated, the spots worked first at exactly the same angle, and the rest of the stitching 'flooded' in around the spots to complete the leaf. See Stitch Variations, Dalmatian dog technique, page 94.

Many woodland flowers are apparently complex, and require careful analysis before stitching begins. This is often best undertaken at the drawing board stage of design. Whilst a simple, semi-stylised study such as Plate 22 at first appears to need no special attention, some elements may require extra study. To create an effectively three-dimensional impression on the blackberries, for instance, it is worth noting that each fruit consists of many separate segments. These should be worked individually, each spherical section at a slightly different angle, and separated by a tiny seed stitch in a contrasting colour. This should be suggested in your initial sketch. More unusual shapes, such as the honeysuckle in Plate 23, the lady's slipper orchid in Plate 24 and the lords and ladies in Plate 25 (Masterclass Four) are also made easier to understand if studied in some detail.

▲ *FIG 17*

Wild clematis, or traveller's joy, is a marvellous motif in embroidery. Suggest the outer extremity of the seed head by transferring a series of tiny dots, working your thread backwards and forwards to build up the fluffy 'old man's beard'. If your thread has a tendency to fragment along its length (or can be encouraged to do so, such as floss silk) allow this to happen, as it will emphasise the fine, cotton boll-like properties of the seed heads. As autumn progresses, the leaves of the clematis turn from green to gold and brown. They often fall before the seeds are fully dispersed by the wind.

'S' is for secret – the secret life of the woodland floor, where many small animals such as wood mice make their home amid the leaf litter, rotten branches and brambles (Rubus fruticosus).

9.5 x 14cm (3¾ x 5½in)

Honeysuckle (*Lonicera periclymenum*) is a beautiful flower (Plate 23). Popular in Art Nouveau design, its country name of 'woodbine' or 'woodbind' hints at the strength of its clockwise climbing habit – so vigorous that it can deform its host's trunk into a barley-sugar twist. The flower heads consist of a number of trumpet-shaped florets, each with a lower and upper lip (see Fig 3, page 7). Depending on the contour of each trumpet, either directional *opus plumarium* or snake stitch should be used (see Stitch Variations, page 93), with radial *opus plumarium* in two strata, falling toward the base of the upper lip, on the front-facing flowers. Long straight stitches, tipped with seed stitches create the stamens. By contrast, the open faces of the lesser periwinkle (*Vinca minor*) suggest a simple splash of colour amid their evergreen foliage.

Honeysuckle and periwinkle both have a long tradition in folklore. Honeysuckle, if brought into the house, meant that a wedding would soon follow, and if a girl slept with honeysuckle in her bedroom, she would dream of love. Periwinkle had rather less pleasant associations – because of its evergreen foliage it was thought to have the properties of immortality. Garlands or crowns of periwinkle were worn by the condemned on their way to execution.

A bank of periwinkle in a woodland setting may well indicate that once a habitation stood at or near the site. An abandoned cottage in the woods falls into ruin more quickly than elsewhere as tree roots erode its foundations, falling branches smash roof and walls and often just a ruined chimney and a heap of overgrown bricks is all that remains of a once neat home. The village washer-woman often ran her business from such an out-of-town location. Trees made excellent posts for her washing line and many woodland plants were used in the laundering process.

◀ *PLATE 23*

In high summer colour spreads through the woods from the ground upward: here, honeysuckle and lesser periwinkles are thrown into relief on a black background. Both plants have simple, lanceolate leaves, bright green and glossy — excellent subjects to practise smoothly sweeping directional opus plumarium. *Work the stem stitched central veins evenly so that the inner edge of the filling stitches can abut them accurately.*

The tiny wren is at home both on the woodland floor and in its canopy, slipping in and out of the tiniest twigs and the most dense vegetation in pursuit of insects.

17.75 x 19cm (7 x 7½in)

▼ *FIG 18*

The spathe (1) of Arum maculatum, *the lords and ladies plant, shrivels after the spadix (2) has encouraged insects to pollinate the female flowers at its base. These mature into extremely poisonous berries (right). Inside each berry is a small round seed, pitted with tiny cavities. The berries cluster tightly along their stem – sketched, they overlap so that only part-spheres are visible. Each berry would be embroidered radially, toward their individual growing point, and a tiny white highlight could be added to suggest the imagined light source, see Plate 17, page 43. If worked on black, careful voiding would be needed.*

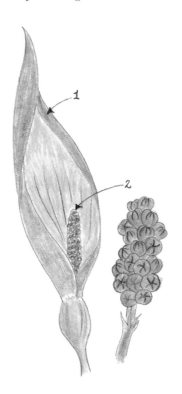

Much less common and more complicated than honeysuckle or periwinkle is the lady's slipper orchid (*Cypripedium calceolus*), only known to grow wild in Britain at one carefully protected site (Plate 24). Perhaps its association in the medieval mind with witchcraft marked it out for persecution, and its rarity value made it a sought-after trophy for Victorian plant collectors. Whatever the reason it is now one of Britain's rarest species, though still widespread in central and northern Europe, favouring limestone woodland.

As an exercise in directional stitching this orchid is peerless! The 'slipper' created by the lower lobe of the flower head curves inward as though pulled together like a drawstring bag. Work several ranks of directional *opus plumarium* between the defining shadow lines to suggest this sweep. Long radial and directional stitches suggest the outer petals and protective leaflet.

Plate 25, our fourth Masterclass project, features two plants used during the Elizabethan period for the starch content of their roots. Bluebells (*Hyacinthoides non-scripta*) and lords and ladies (*Arum maculatum*) were used to stiffen the elaborate ruffs of the aristocracy. Sweet violets (*Viola odorata*) were strewn on floors and amongst linens to sweeten the musty odours of less sanitary days. With the pretty lilac-veined flowers of the wood-sorrel (*Oxalis acetosella*) these plants make an atmospheric study of the woodland floor.

In the Middle Ages, the strangely shaped lords and ladies was inextricably linked with the act of making love. Its common names all supported the association: 'silly lovers', 'Adam and Eve' and 'Cuckoo pintle' – the latter from cuckold, a man whose wife has been unfaithful. Its anatomy makes the analogy obvious (Fig 18). The flowers, both male and female, are enclosed within a broad, sheathing hood called the spathe. Inside there is a club-like structure (the spadix) giving off a slight warmth which, together with a musky smell, attracts insects which pollinate the flowers. Smoothly worked, carefully angled directional *opus plumarium* describes the spathe, and by leaving a discreet void between the inner edge of this stitching and the seed stitched spadix, a truly three-dimensional effect can be achieved. The broad, spectacular leaf is worked in Dalmatian dog technique.

Delicate use of opposite angle stitching is essential to capture the upturned tips of the bluebell caps, called 'crowtoes' in the sixteenth century. The sepals are worked in directional stitching, or occasionally snake stitch (see Stitch Variations, page 93). This would apply equally to an embroidery of the columbine shown below in Fig 19. An analysis of each campanile reveals that both sepals and petals share the same deep blue colour making the once common bluebell one of springtime's most attractive flowers. Both these complex structures are complemented by the regular faces and simple foliage of the violets and the trefoil leaves of the wood-sorrel.

The rich, mulched structure of the forest floor, with its leaf debris and dappled light suggests that any study designed to capture its atmosphere should share something of its diversity of plant life. In Masterclass Four we explore four very different plants each presenting unusual shapes and textures.

▲ *PLATE 24*

The lady's slipper orchid, a rare and beautiful plant, makes a striking and unusual portrait. The dull purple outer petals reflex and curve elegantly, making the use of opposite angle embroidery essential to capture their flexible appearance. Careful shadow lining on the 'slipper', together with directional stitching and a field of deep grey radial work to suggest the inner void of the lower lobe makes this a complex subject. The leaves (not shown here) are broad, oval and strongly veined and should be approached similarly to the leaves of the ribwort plantain discussed in Chapter Three, page 43.

6.25 x 9cm (2½ x 3½ in)

FIG 19

The dusky purple flowers of the columbine (Aquilegia vulgaris) form a complicated motif. The long spurs at the base of each compound petal secrete nectar which is collected by long-tongued bumble bees, in similar fashion to the honeysuckle trumpets. They could also be worked similarly, each spur in snake or directional stitching as appropriate (see Plate 23). Seen from below (bottom) the anatomy of the flower falling back towards its central core is evident. Once this is established, it should be easy to work the profile and semi-profile flowers correctly.

THE WOODLAND FLOOR IN SPRING

Blues, violets and purples intermingle with both deep and delicate shades of green to capture

the magic of spring woodlands. The irregular pyramidal structure of the design leads

the eye from the forest floor, where sinuous shapes intertwine, up into the stately campanile

of the bluebells, suggesting the various plants' efforts to reach light amid the trees.

Worked here on a creamy fabric, a pale green material might also be a successful backdrop to this study, or a pale, peachy shade such as in Plate 22. Trace off the design and transfer it onto your fabric as usual, being particularly careful not to omit any of the fine details on the bluebells, or the spots on the leaf of the lords and ladies. Always make sure that you have left enough fabric around the edge of your design to allow for the final

TECHNIQUES

Apart from a broadening of stem stitch into snake stitch
(see Stitch Variations, page 93) the only new development in our
work for this project is Dalmatian dog technique:

Stem stitch • Shooting stitch • *Opus plumarium*

Seed stitch • Snake stitch • Dalmatian dog technique

presentation process (see page 91). Mount the fabric into your tambour frame.

You may find it useful to re-cap on the principles of directional *opus plumarium* in the Stitch Variations section (page 93) before beginning Dalmatian dog technique.

PLATE 25 ▶

Masterclass Four: Embroidery shown life size 19 x 21.5cm (7½ x 8½in)

HELEN M
STEVENS

Carefully transfer the design onto your background material using the template shown (see Basic Techniques, page 90). Make sure that you have included all of the details featured before you begin stitching.

SUGGESTED COLOURS

1 Black
2 Leaf green
3 Bright green
4 Soft green
5 Very pale green
6 Deep blue
7 Sky blue
8 Ice blue
9 White
10 Violet
11 Orange
12 Dark green
13 Deep beige
14 Dull purple

Select your colours referring to the colour chart and Plate 25. The tones of the blue threads should be very 'true' from deep, through to paler and finally ice blue to achieve a natural effect. The purple chosen for the lords and ladies should be rather dull. Remember that the names afforded to the various colours in the colour chart are suggestions for ease of reference and not necessarily representative of your final choice.

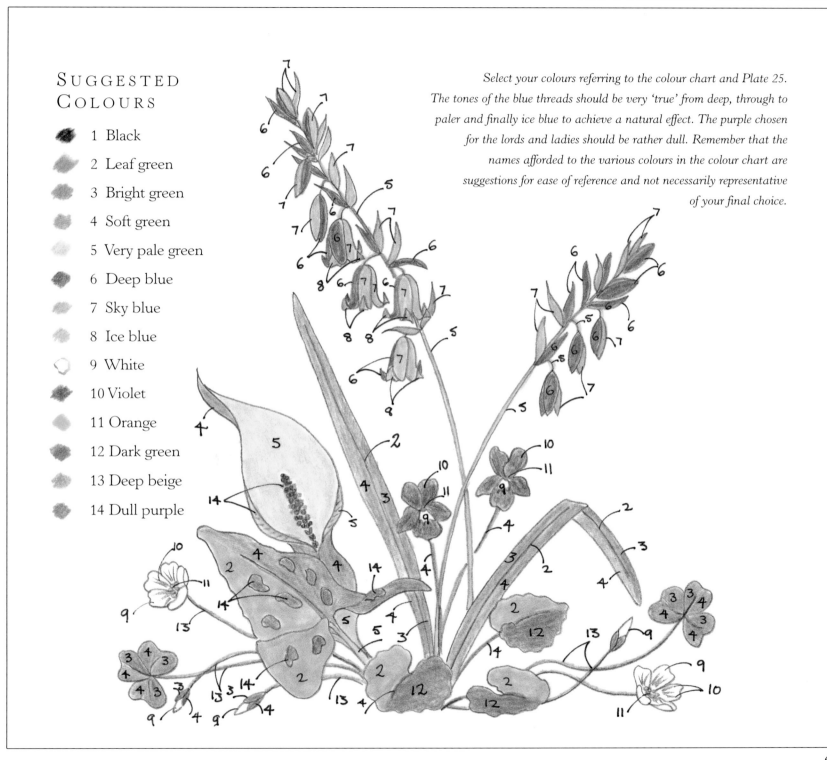

DESIGN NOTES

To create the effect of the dappled sunlight of the woods, the imagined light source within this study is somewhat diffuse. Whilst generally it is seen to filter in from above, scattered reflections and the movement of the leaves means that your shadow line will be less uniformly on only one side of each motif. Study Plate 25 carefully, and suggest your shadow lines accordingly in black (1).

START WITH THE BLUEBELLS...

Work the central veins of the leaves in narrow stem stitch in leaf green (2), and the leaves themselves in smooth fields of directional *opus plumarium* sloping fairly acutely toward their elongated core in bright green (3) and soft green (4). Now move on to the buds and flowers.

1 Work the stem in very pale green (5) in narrow and then broad stem stitch beginning at the top, graduating to simple snake stitch (see Stitch Variations, page 93) as they become broader toward the base (see Plate 25). Work the immature and opening buds in lozenges and part lozenges of radial and directional *opus plumarium* as appropriate in deep blue (6) and sky blue (7). Complete the sepals in the indicated shades in radial or directional *opus plumarium* or, in the case of the lowest sepal, reflexing snake stitch (Stitch Variations, page 93).

2 Embroider the stem and various buds and sepals as described in step 1.

Work the main field of each petal on the open bells in deep or sky blue:

Topmost of the four flowers, work the central petal in radial *opus plumarium*, the stitches angled toward the flower stalk.

Second down, complete the central petal, and add the left-hand petal in directional *opus plumarium*.

Third down, add the right-hand petal similarly.

Work the up-turned tips of the bells in ice blue (8) in very small single strata of radial *opus plumarium*, using the opposite angle principle, as shown on the bottom flower.

3 Work the flower stalks and stems of the sweet violets in narrow stem stitch in soft green.

Work a narrow inner strata of radial *opus plumarium* in white (9) on the lower petal of each flower, followed by an outer strata in violet (10) shown on the right-hand flower. Lateral and upper petals are worked in single strata of violet (left) and two small seed stitches slipped into the centre of each flower in orange (11).

4 Work the central veins and leaf stems of the violets in narrow stem stitch in soft green (upper leaf). Sweep broad arcs of directional *opus plumarium* in leaf green and dark green (12) from the tip of each leaf to its base, following the central vein and advancing the angle sharply as you approach the base (middle and left).

5 Using fine stem stitch and fine reflexing stem stitch, work the stems, stalks and leaf veins of the wood-sorrel in deep beige (13).

Complete the buds in lozenges and part lozenges of radial *opus plumarium* in white, bright green and soft green.

Work the upper and lower lobes of the trefoil leaves in the appropriate shades in directional *opus plumarium*.

Following the principles of radial and opposite angle stitching, complete the flower petals in white, and work the shooting stitches in violet. Seed stitches in orange form the pollen masses at the centre of the flowers.

MOVING ON TO THE LORDS AND LADIES...

6 Work the spadix of the flower in closely packed seed stitch in dull purple (14).

In one very long radial strata of *opus plumarium*, complete the inner surface of the spathe in very pale green. In the same shade, using opposite angle embroidery, work the small reflexed areas on either side of the spathe, incorporating a few shooting stitches in dull purple. In reflexing snake stitch, work the tip of the spathe in soft green, and the base of the spathe in directional *opus plumarium*.

7 Carefully analyse the directional stitching on each section of the leaf and work the central vein in graduating stem stitch in very pale green.

Work the spots in dull purple. Flood the large fields of the upper and lower sides of the leaf with broad arcs of directional *opus plumarium* (soft green and leaf green, respectively), allowing

the spots to interrupt the flow of stitching where necessary, but keeping the angles constant.

Repeat the process for the areas of the leaf worked in opposite angle embroidery. Complete the small fields on the underside of the leaf in directional stitching in the appropriate shades.

CHAPTER FIVE

THE RIVERSIDE

A shimmering blue stream like fine gauze in the sunlight, delicate white water-plants bobbing in

the current and a vibrant flash of silky turquoise feathers as a kingfisher darts across his

territory – the river runs deep and cool beneath its overhanging fringe of shrubs and flowers.

Tiny, bright stars in pastel shades or sunbursts of vivid primary colours, tall and sinuous

or low-lying: its plant life offers inspiration both innovative and interpretative.

lowland river is the aquatic equivalent of ancient woodland, but its maturity is attained not through years alone but also over miles. From its source it will pass through many types of soils, gathering nutrients to feed a variety of life, and eventually even a fast stream will slow to a more sedate flow. In the mainstream at the centre of the river where the current flows fastest, long-stemmed, trailing plants flourish; at its shallow, slower paced edges, the habitat becomes almost equivalent to a lake, sharing its more upright, vigorous flora.

In Plate 26 the thread-like lower leaves of the common water-crowfoot (*Ranunculus aquatilis*) break through the water's surface suggesting the sub-aquatic world below. Its bright yellow and white buttercup-like flowers can mass into striking carpets of blooms, as can fringed water lilies (*Nymphoides peltata*) (Fig 20).

At the water's edge many plants mingle. The highly efficient seed dispersal system of the common dandelion (*Taraxacum officinale*) means that it has colonised almost every habitat, including the riverside. Though common, and often despised as an invasive weed on cultivated land, there can be no denying the decorative qualities of the dandelion's gossamer-fine globe, the 'clock' so beloved of generations of children who have told the

◄ *PLATE 26*

The shades used for the landscape and foreground elements here have been carefully chosen to blend together and enhance each other. Only the kingfisher is worked in vibrant colours from a separate palette. The result is startlingly three-dimensional: the bird seems to skim across the surface of the water in a flash of vivid movement.

From the left, clockwise: common dandelion, water plantain, water lily, common water-crowfoot and multicoloured duckweed (Lemna gibba) floating on the surface of the foreground water.
Embroidery shown life size
24 x 20.25cm (9½ x 8in)

time by blowing away the 200 or more seeds on every head, each borne aloft by its own tiny parachute. Work each parachute as a miniature 'sunburst' of straight stitches in your finest thread. Build up the globe around a central core of seed stitches and attach the outermost parachutes to their seeds by straight stitches creating long 'necks'. The structure of these 'whole' seeds can be seen on those blowing away in Plate 26.

Less common and equally attractive are the pretty lilac flowers of the water plantain (*Alisma plantago-aquatica*). Each delicate flower remains closed all morning, opens during the afternoon and closes again in the early evening. Along the much-punted reaches of the River Cam, I once heard Cambridge students refer to them as 'lazy dons'.

Offering a complete contrast to the fine tracery of the plantain, the white water lily (*Nymphaea alba*) with its striking many-petalled bowl and fleshy leaves is a plant of slow moving or still waters. Its broad, almost circular leaves float on the surface of the stream, occasionally gathering pockets of water at their centre. This can be suggested by overlaying horizontal stitches on the underlying radial *opus plumarium*, effectively returning the eye to the low perspective of the water's surface.

Plate 26 shows that by contrasting the textures of the foreground features (floss silk) with those of the background (twisted silk and cottons) the effect of looking 'through' a window of living subjects at the landscape beyond is emphasised. Within that distant microcosm only the kingfisher and the trees and irises at the water's edge are worked in floss silk, again as a way of drawing the eye deeper into the picture. The sky – another dimension – is worked in very fine strands of untwisted silk, its colours reflected in the twisted silk of the water.

Plate 27 takes us one step further. The water violet (*Hottonia palustris*) has no leaves on its upper stem. Beneath the water fine whorls of waving, weed-like tendrils serve as hiding places for tiny water fleas and daphnia. To emphasise the water's movement work the leaves in bright shades of fine green stem stitch, allowing the tendrils to curve and overlap randomly. The cellophane thread, separated from a combined blending filament,

▲ *FIG 20*

The fringed water lily is a pleasingly simple water plant. The flower lacks the complicated many-petalled structure of the white water lily, and presents an open face, easily worked in radial opus plumarium. *The leaves are very similar to the lily pads of other species. Whilst it is useful at sketch-book stage to suggest an indication of the water itself, do not transfer this onto the background fabric. Water should be worked freehand and allowed to 'flow' freely until you are satisfied with the result: this is rarely as you envisage it in sketch form.*

worked over and through the other features catches and reflects external light to enhance the shimmering, watery effect. Very long straight stitches separate the dimensions above and below the water.

Above, the violet flower heads intertwine with another sinuous plant of the shallows, the water forget-me-not (*Myosotis scorpiodes*). As its Latin name suggests, the arched flower head of this lovely little plant lengthens gradually as its blooms open, looking like a scorpion's tail. This is a habit shared by several water loving (though not strictly aquatic) plants, including common and rough comfrey (Fig 21). The latter also shares its subtle variation of colouring – the closed buds are pink, gradually turning blue as they open. Both the water violet and the forget-me-not have long stems which should be

PLATE 27 ▶

To capture the twin dimensions of above and
below the water, a long, slim format works well,
here on a ratio of around 1:2. Setting the waterline
about two-thirds of the way down suggests that
there is much more 'space' above the water than
below. A breeze blowing across the water is implied
by the overall sweep of the plants to the right,
whilst their individual curves incline to the left.
The lower flowers of the water violet have collected
a few drops of water with the sideways movement,
which drips back down to the surface.
12.5 x 25.5cm (5 x 10in)

▲ *FIG 21*

Common comfrey (Symphytum officinale) *(left)
and rough comfrey* (S. asperum) *are tall,
branched plants with nodding, bell-like flowers.
Whilst the petals do not reflex as acutely as
those of the bluebells in Masterclass Four, they
should be approached in the same way and be
carefully shadow lined. The stems and leaves are
slightly bristly – achieved by using two shades in
the needle, as for the downy undersides of the great
mullein in Plate 16 (page 40). Folk names for
comfrey include 'knit-bone' as the roots, ground
up and made into a sludge with water, hardens
like plaster-of-Paris and was used by medieval
herbalists to set bones.*

worked in fine, slightly graduating and reflexing stem stitch. Their flowers are simple, falling away to a central core and should be worked in fine strata of radial *opus plumarium*. These plants are used as shelter for three-spined sticklebacks, which are among the smallest freshwater fish in Britain. Preferring slow running water, they shun the centre of fast streams, using the foliage of shallow-growing plants to build nests in which they care for their young during the first few weeks of life.

Flowers in the far distance (along the water's edge in Plate 26 for instance) can be worked using various impressionist tricks. Long, upright, slightly slanted straight stitches suggest the leaves and stems. The flower heads (in this case yellow irises) are simply indicated by three converging seed stitches, perhaps emphasised by a second inner colour, and single seed stitches creating buds. As the flowers recede into the still further distance even these details merge, as mere dots and dashes of colour are enough to lead the eye away into the rest of the scene.

Where flowers form a middle distance feature, however, such as in Plate 28 or as suggested by Fig 22, the principles of close-up work still apply. The stately swans and their cygnet need to be framed by features which will set the perspective of the piece. The bluebells should be worked as explored in Masterclass Four, and the primroses following the familiar rules of radial and directional *opus plumarium*. Remember that subjects closer to the viewer may appear to cross the eyeline and overlap background features. Shallows of the water are worked first and the grasses worked over them. Be careful not to pull the underlying stitches out of shape as the subsequent work is overlaid. The weeping willow leaves and catkins are also placed into the foreground by allowing them to cross the field of the water.

Working in close-up on black, the principles of perspective must be suggested by voiding. In Plate 29 the overlapping flowers of the arrowhead plant (*Sagittaria sagittifolia*), together with their arching buds, are separated by careful voiding – particularly effective as the black background divides the white petals. Arrowhead is related to the water plantain

◄ *PLATE 28*

What could be more tranquil on a spring afternoon than the peaceful presence of swans? The lessons we have learned interpreting flower and foliage forms will eventually lead to an understanding of the techniques needed to convey the whole of a scene such as this. Opus plumarium, *as we have discussed, translates as 'feather work': the stitched plumage of the swans feathers out and falls back towards its core, and the stubby feathers of the cygnet are worked on similar principles.*
19 x 16cm (7½ x 6½in)

◄ *FIG 22*

*Rather dull in close up, bulrushes (*Typha latifolia*) make an attractive middle-distance feature, and could be used in a scene such as Plate 28. Alice, in her journey though the looking glass, tried to gather armfuls of bulrushes only to find them melt away into her dream. The thousands of seeds borne away on fluffy parachutes when the female flower matures do, indeed, seem to melt away as they disperse. As landscape features, these motifs should be worked in fine thread, shadow lined if on a pale background, with a suggestion of water or long grasses at their base.*

▼ *PLATE 29*

Like the roundels in Plates 5, 11 and 21, this smaller design draws the eye around the picture in an endless circle of frog, mayfly and arrowhead, with the main element, the frog, emphasised by outlining in surface couched gold thread.
10.75 x 12cm (4¼ x 4¾in)

and bears flowers of both sexes. The white, upper flowers are male, the lower, bur-like heads, female. Radial *opus plumarium*, shot through with deep purple tracery and completed by seed stitches in metallic gold thread describe the former. The female flowers are more delicate. Green sepals worked according to the opposite angle principle support the reproductive organs, worked in long straight stitches in fine metallic gold and tipped by tiny seed stitches in dull purple.

In Plate 29 (as in Plate 27), the main protagonist is emphasised by outlining in surface-couched gold thread. Surface couching allows the main thread to lie smoothly on the background fabric as it is caught down by the couching thread (see Stitch Variations, page 94). It can both separate features, as it is used here to differentiate between the planes of stitching, or can create a feature in its own right, as in Plate 30 (page 81) where it is used as the central vein in the iris leaves and to create coiling arabesques. The long tail filaments of the mayfly are worked in a finer gauge of gold metallic thread, in straight stitches through the background fabric.

Metallic threads are an effective addition to an embroiderer's palette and whether used to give a fine fillip and sparkle to a delicate subject or more dramatically to highlight a bold subject their gauge should be chosen carefully to fulfil each specific purpose (see Materials, page 88). Fine metallic threads (usually faux gold or silver) can be threaded onto a suitable needle and worked through the fabric in the usual way. Thicker threads, such as heavy passing or Jap gold, should be applied to the surface of the work only – the most effective method for naturalistic purposes is couching (see Stitch Variations, page 94). In Plates 27 and 29 it is used to outline the fish and frog respectively. In our final Masterclass project it is used on the leaves of the iris and to suggest decorative features.

Tall, stately plants at the water's edge have been chosen as the subjects for Masterclass Five (Plate 30, page 81). Left to right, the flowering rush (*Butomus umbellatus*), yellow flag iris (*Iris pseudacorus*) and bur-reed (*Sparganium emersum*) present a variety of flower types which all require careful interpretation of techniques already explored. The upturned umbrella spokes of the flowering rush bear magnificent dark-veined pink flowers in similar shades to the willowherb (Fig 23). The yellow flag iris has large petals requiring the confident use of broad swathes of *opus plumarium*. The male (upper) and female (lower) flowers of the bur-reed are worked in straight and seed stitching.

To the right of the study, a mayfly is an optional addition to the design. Along the river, insect and animal life abound. Each embroidery in this chapter has included bird, animal, fish or insect (sometimes more than one!) and although the projects in this book have concentrated upon flowers, the techniques which we have mastered are fundamental to creating embroideries which will ultimately allow you to capture all these subjects. Shadow lining and voiding are necessary parts of all pictorial embroideries in this style. The sweeping stitches which we have used on petals and leaves can also convey fur and feather. Straight and seed stitching, Dalmatian dog spotting, chevron and shooting techniques can create butterfly wings, animal whiskers, bird plumage – even landscapes and portraits.

Embroidery is an art for all seasons, all subjects and all lovers of nature and the natural world.

▲ *FIG 23*

Great willowherb (Epilobium hirsutum) (left), and its cousin marsh willowherb (E. palustre) is found by the side of rivers, marshes and in fenland throughout Britain. It even enjoys the sluggish flow of field-side ditches. It is one of the easiest plants to find and identify, its simple four-petalled flowers and lance-shaped leaves make it easy to sketch and use as an original design. It is deeply satisfying to work an embroidery from your own drawing, so don't be afraid to try. Draughtsmanship is a skill which can be acquired and need not be the result of natural talent!

PLANTS OF THE RIVER BANK

Our last Masterclass features tall, stately aristocrats of the stream's edge. Colours are vibrant and striking, stitching bold yet detailed and the style of the piece naturalistic but with a twist of stylised drama. Gold thread twines around the lower stems of the plants suggesting the tangled mass of low growing plants which would otherwise complicate the base of the design.

The mayfly to the right of the pattern could be omitted, or moved into another area of the design. To change the dimensions of the piece, it could be positioned above and to the left of the flowering rush, and the stems of each plant lengthened, following the sweep of curve already established, creating an elegant, slim design similar to Plate 27. How you interpret these designs is *your* choice.

Trace off the design, or alter it as you wish, and transfer onto your fabric. Select your colours and metallic thread, referring to the notes in Materials, page 88. If you use a plied gold thread, split some of it down into its component filaments before you begin work, and wind these separately onto a card. You can then cut off small lengths of a single strand as necessary.

TECHNIQUES

With the addition of surface couching, this design is worked entirely in techniques we have already explored:

Stem stitch • *Opus plumarium*
Straight stitch • Shooting stitch • Snake stitch
Surface couching • Seed stitch

PLATE 30 ▶
Masterclass Five: Embroidery shown life size 19.5 x 21.5cm (7¾ x 8½in)

HELEN M
STEVENS

Carefully transfer the design onto your background material using the template here (see Basic Techniques, page 90). Make sure that you have included all of the details featured before you begin stitching.

SUGGESTED COLOURS

1 Yellow green

2 Leaf green

3 Bright yellow

4 Pale orange

5 Deep yellow

6 Dark purple

7 Rhubarb pink

8 Pink

9 Deep pink

10 Golden brown

11 Bright green

12 White

13 Metallic gold

DESIGN NOTES

The design is shown worked on a black background, but could be successful on a pale base, in which case shadow lining should be included to indicate an internal light source from the top right-hand quadrant. On black, or any other dark colour chosen, be especially careful to void accurately, particularly between the complicated structures of the iris petals.

BEGIN WITH THE FLAG IRIS...

For the flower stem and blooms work the strong, upright stem in snake stitch following the direction of the curve in yellow green (1).

1 In yellow green and leaf green (2) work the bract-like protective leaf at the base of the bud in radial and directional *opus plumarium*, as appropriate, and the sepal of the

bud itself in yellow green radial *opus plumarium*. In directional *opus plumarium* complete the closed petals of the bud in bright yellow (3). Leaving a voided break to suggest the 'rip', work the tear-drop shaped protective leaf below the main flower in a single strata of radial *opus plumarium* in leaf green.

2 The petal structure is complex, with three large lower petals or 'falls', and six smaller 'standards' at the centre. Beginning with the falls, work an inner strata of radial *opus plumarium* in pale orange (4), as shown on the right-hand petal, followed by a long outer strata in mixed threads of bright yellow and deep yellow (5), shown to the left of the centre petal. Work long shooting stitches in dark purple (6) from the inner edge outward to a point just beyond the meeting of the strata. Complete the reflexed areas in opposite angle stitching in bright and deep yellow as appropriate.

3 Now move on to the standards, of which three
   are upright and smooth, and three flexed and
feathery. Work the standards in deep yellow
directional *opus plumarium* (bright yellow where
reflexed). On the feathery standards only, work
shooting stitches in fine metallic gold (13) following
the same directional flow.

MOVING ON TO THE FLOWERING RUSH...

4 Complete each flower stalk in narrow stem stitch in rhubarb pink
   (7) and the buds in lozenges and part lozenges of rhubarb pink
and pink (8) in radial and directional *opus plumarium* as indicated.

   Work the flower sepals in rhubarb pink radial *opus plumarium* (top),
and the reflexed areas in opposite angle stitching (centre and bottom).

   Similarly, work the petals in pink (centre) and add shooting stitches
in deep pink (9).

   Complete the pollen masses in seed stitches of deep pink and
metallic gold thread (bottom).

   Work the protective bracts in golden brown (10) arcs of directional
opus plumarium.

5 Work the long stem of the flowering rush in smooth snake stitch in golden brown.

The long, linear leaves of the iris (to the extreme left and second right of the overall design) have prominent central veins. These will be added later (see step 6). Work each side of the leaves (reflexed as necessary) in smooth arcs of directional *opus plumarium* in yellow green and leaf green, leaving the line of the central vein voided.

MOVING ON TO THE BUR-REED...

6 Work the upper three male flowers of the bur-reed in seed stitched pale orange. The lower three should be worked with an inner core of seed stitches in leaf green, and an outer corolla in pale orange, some of the pale orange seed stitches overlapping and mingling with the leaf green.

7 The female bur-reed flowers are worked in
straight stitch. Work leaf green at the centre
of each flower, falling roughly to an inner core (top),
overlay this with pale orange (middle), and finally
with very fine white (12) (bottom).
Work the inner surfaces of the leaves in leaf green
directional or radial *opus plumarium*, and the outer
surfaces in bright green (11) snake stitch. Allowing
the leaves to merge into them, continue the snake
stitch downwards to complete the stems.
Carefully following the transferred line, surface
couch thick metallic gold thread to create the decorative tendrils, laying two threads side
by side where indicated (see Plate 30 page 81 and colour chart page 83). Similarly, couch
gold metallic thread to create the central veins of the iris leaves.

8 The mayfly is optional. Work the segmented body of
the mayfly in closely packed straight stitches in golden
brown. In your finest white thread work the wings in radial
stitches, falling toward the body of the insect, allowing a
little of the background fabric to show between each stitch.
In long and short straight stitches complete the legs in
golden brown and the antennae and long tail filaments in
fine metallic gold.

MATERIALS

FABRIC

The choice of fabric and threads can affect the ultimate appearance of any embroidery and, as with the choice of colourways, should be at the discretion of the embroiderer. However, to achieve satisfactory results, certain practical considerations need to be borne in mind.

For so-called flat-work embroidery which must be worked in a frame, it is essential that the fabric chosen for the background does not stretch. If the fabric stretches even slightly while the embroidery is in progress, when taken out of the frame it will contract to its normal size and the embroidery will be distorted. It is also a good idea to look for a smooth, evenweave fabric. Suitable fabrics include:

* Cotton
* Polyester cotton ('Percale')
* Linen

Pure silk may also be used, but avoid types with too much 'slub' in the weave as this will interrupt the flow of the embroidery stitches.

The embroideries in this book have been worked upon an inexpensive cotton/polyester fabric (sometimes called 'Percale') which is very lightweight. Poly-cotton mixes (evenweave) in a heavier weight are also ideal for use in this type of embroidery. Larger pictures should be worked on heavier fabrics, small studies on

lightweights, but this rule can be adapted to the particular needs of the work in question.

When choosing fabric, try to avoid any fabrics which have too loose a weave, as this will result in too many stitches vying for space in too few threads of warp and weft. As a general rule, if the weave is open enough to be used for counted thread embroidery, it will be too wide for us!

THREADS

A variety of threads are necessary to achieve diverse effects but the ultimate choice of which type to use on any specific area is a personal one. Any thread suitable for 'flatwork' embroidery may be used for any of the techniques in this book. Natural fibres are easier to use than synthetics and include cotton, floss silk and twisted silk.

Pure silks and cottons are available in a glorious variety of colours and textures. Clockwise from bottom left: stranded cottons, stranded and twisted silks, Japanese floss silk, fine floss silk, spun (fine twisted) silk.

✻ COTTON
Most embroiderers are familiar with stranded cotton. It is usually available in six-stranded skeins and strands should be used singly.

✻ FLOSS SILK
This is untwisted with a high sheen, and is also known as sleave or Japanese silk. It should be doubled or split (as appropriate to the type chosen) to match the gauge of a single strand of stranded cotton to complete most of the projects in this book.

✻ TWISTED SILK
This usually has several strands twisted together. Single strands of most twisted silks are approximately the same gauge as single strands of stranded cotton and should be used singly. Very fine details should be worked in finer gauges of thread if available.

✻ SYNTHETIC METALLIC THREADS
These are available in many formats in gold, silver and various other colours. The most versatile are several stranded threads which may be used entire where a thick gauge is required, or split into single strands for fine or delicate details.

✳ 'REAL' GOLD AND SILVER THREAD
These threads are usually made using a percentage of real gold or silver. Generally they comprise very narrow strips of leaf or fine metal twisted around a synthetic, cotton or silk core. 'Passing' thread is tightly wound and available in various gauges, the finest of which may be used directly in the needle, the thicker couched down. 'Jap' gold is more loosely wound, is also available in a variety of gauges, but is usually only suitable for couching.

✳ BLENDING FILAMENTS
This term encompasses a vast number of specialist threads, but usually refers to threads which are made up of a number of strands of differing types, e.g. a silky thread together with a cellophane or sparkling thread. They may be used entire, or split down into their component parts which may be used separately.

TOOLS

Basic embroidery tools have remained unchanged for centuries and the essentials are described here.

✳ EMBROIDERY FRAME
In flat embroidery the tension of the background fabric is all important (see Stitch Variations, page 92) and it is essential to work on an embroidery frame. Round, tambour hoops are best suited to fine embroidery as they produce an entirely uniform tension. Wooden hoops maintain their tension best. Always use a frame large enough to allow a generous amount of fabric around your design.

✳ SCISSORS
You will need small scissors for threads, fine and sharp. I use pinking shears for cutting fabric, which also helps to prevent fraying. Don't use thread or fabric scissors to cut anything else or you will blunt the blades.

✳ NEEDLES
These should always be chosen with the specific use of threads and fabrics in mind. 'Embroidery' needles are designed with a long eye and a sharp point. A selection of sizes 5 to 10 are the most useful. Size 8 is ideal for use with a 'single strand' gauge as discussed above.

▼ *Floss and twisted silk produce different effects: glossy, as shown on the plant and upper sides of the butterflies' wings, or with the subtler, matt glow illustrated by the underside of the wings.*
10.75 x 12.75cm (4½ x 5in)

▲ *Metallic and specialist materials. Clockwise from top left: imitation gold thread (stranded), real gold passing thread, coloured metallic threads, real silver passing thread, blending filaments, imitation silver thread (stranded) with bugle and seed beads.*

▲ *Working in stranded cotton and imitation metallic thread can create a soft, muted effect.*
10 x 12.75cm (4 x 5in)

BASIC TECHNIQUES

Before you begin to embroider it is important to pay attention to the initial preparation and transfer of your design. Similarly, after your project is completed you need to give some thought to the presentation of the work.

TRANSFERRING A DESIGN

You will need (see picture above, left to right):

* Original design
* Tracing paper (use good quality 90gsm)
* 'H' pencil
* Drawing pins

* Dressmakers' carbon paper in a colour contrasting your fabric
* Fabric
* Tissue paper
* Tambour hoop

You will also need scissors and a smooth, hard surface on which to work. Ideally, this should be a wooden drawing board covered with several layers of lining paper.

1 Place the tracing paper over your design and carefully trace off the design, omitting any very fine details, e.g., whiskers, spiders' webs, butterflies' antennae. These lines, if transferred, could not be covered by single strands of thread and must be added freehand during the course of the embroidery.

2 Lay your fabric flat, and place the tracing on top of it. Pin the tracing in place with two drawing pins at the top right and left-hand corners. Interleave between fabric and tracing

with the carbon (colour side down) and hold secure with a third pin through the tracing at the bottom of the paper. Do not pin through the carbon.

With a firm, even pressure, re-draw each line of the design. After you have completed a few lines, lift one corner of the tracing and carbon papers to check that the design is transferring successfully.

3 When the transfer is complete, remove the bottom drawing pin, lift back the tracing and remove the carbon paper. Check that every detail has been

transferred before finally removing the tracing paper. You are now ready to mount your fabric, using tissue paper and a tambour hoop (see instructions opposite).

MOUNTING FABRIC IN A TAMBOUR HOOP

You will need:
* Fabric, with the design transferred
* Tissue paper
* Tambour hoop

1 Cut two sheets of tissue paper at least 5cm (2in) wider than the outer dimensions of your tambour hoop. Place the inner ring of your hoop on a flat surface and lay one sheet of tissue

paper over it. Lay your fabric over the tissue paper, and ensure that the design is centred in the ring. Lay a second sheet of tissue paper over the fabric and slip the outer ring of the hoop over the entire 'sandwich'. Tighten the screw until the fabric and paper is held firmly.

2 Trim the upper sheet of tissue paper inside and outside the upper ring (shown above). Turn the hoop over and trim the lower sheet of tissue paper similarly. The tissue paper will protect your fabric from abrasion by the hoop and keep the handled edges clean. You are now ready to begin your embroidery.

MOUNTING AND FRAMING YOUR WORK

You will need (see picture above):
* Backing board (rigid cardboard, foamboard or hardboard)
* Acid free cartridge paper (cut to the same size as the backing board)
* Lacing thread (mercerised cotton is recommended)
* Two crewel needles (large enough to take the chosen cotton)
* Scissors

1 When your embroidery is complete press it on the wrong side, without steam (after checking the manufacturer's instructions for fabric and thread). Always press through another piece of fabric, and be *particularly* careful if you have used blending or other specialist filaments, especially cellophane threads.

It is essential to mount your work under similar tension to that exerted upon the fabric whilst in the tambour hoop. Lace it firmly onto a rigid backing board to achieve this tension. Make sure your backing board is large enough to take the whole design, with enough space at each edge to allow for framing.

2 Place the cartridge paper carefully between the board and the fabric. Next, position your embroidery, always making sure that the warp/left of the fabric lies straight in relation the edges of the board.

3 Invert the ensemble so that the embroidery is face down, with the cartridge paper and board on top of it. Cut the fabric to size, allowing a comfortable overlap. Fold the two sides in toward the centre of the board. Cut a long but manageable piece of lacing thread and thread a needle at each end, leaving two 'tails', of similar length.

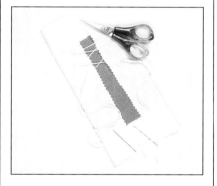

Working from the top, insert a needle on either side and lace the two sides of the fabric together, in corset fashion, until you reach the bottom. If you run out of thread simply tie the thread off and begin again.

4 Fold the top and bottom of the fabric toward the centre and repeat the lacing process. Always tie off the ends of the lacing thread with firm, non-slip knots and snip off any extra thread which is left. It takes a little

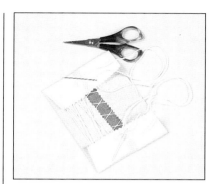

practise to achieve the perfect tension. Do not over tighten the laces as the thread may break, or rip the fabric, but do not be afraid to exert a reasonable pull on the work as only in this way will the original tension of the fabric on the tambour hoop be re-created.

5 The choice of framing is a personal matter, but always be prepared to take professional advice as framing can make or mar a picture. A window mount is a good idea to keep the glass away from the fabric (essential if beads or thick specialist threads have been used) and remember that a frame should complement rather than dominate your design.

STITCH VARIATIONS

The stitches in this book are a combination of traditional embroidery stitches and contemporary innovations. They are flexible and adaptable: a single basic stitch such as stem stitch, depending on how it is applied, can produce a variety of effects, from a fine, sinuous line to a broad, strong one, with an infinite choice of widths, curves and reflexes within each variation.

The stitches fall into several distinct categories: linear, filling and decorative. Each has its own special properties and is suited to the description of certain shapes, fields and textures.

When working on a hoop the fabric *must* be taut within the frame. Stitches are always worked by the 'stab and pull' method. The needle is pushed through the fabric from above, the embroiderer's hand then moves to the back and pulls the needle through the fabric so the stitch forms smoothly on the surface. The next stitch is begun by pushing the needle up through the fabric from the reverse of the work, the hand brought to the front to pull the needle through, prior to beginning the routine once again.

LINEAR STITCHES

1 STEM STITCH

Always work from the top of any line to be described (on a natural history subject the outer extremity). Work *with* the curve of the subject: bring your needle out just to the outside of the curve and put it in on the inside of the curve.

a Fine/narrow stem stitch
Overlap the stitches by only a small proportion of the stitch length. The line created is only the width of a single stitch, creating a fine, sinuous effect.

b Broad stem stitch
Overlap the stitches so that half to three-quarters of each stitch lies beside its neighbour. The juxtaposition of several stitches creates a thick, strong effect.

c Graduating stem stitch
Begin with a fine stem stitch, increase it to a one-half ratio, then to three-quarters ratio within the same line creating the effect of a gradually thickening line (such as describes a growing stem – narrower at the tip, broader at the base).

d Coiling stem stitch
Begin with small stitches to describe the tight curve at the centre of the coil and gradually lengthen the stitches as the curve becomes gentler.

e Reflexing stem stitch
Beginning at the tip of the line, work the chosen variation a–c until the direction of the curve begins to change. Take one straight stitch through the preceding stitch, directly along the pattern line. Begin the stem stitch again, bringing the needle up on the new outside of the curve.

2 STRAIGHT STITCH

There are occasions when a completely straight line in the pattern can be described by a simple, straight stitch, or when a large field of the design must be filled smoothly with abutting straight stitches, such as in landscape work. The fabric must be taut within your frame to work this technique successfully.

a Vertical straight stitch (long)
Work this stitch from the top downward. Usually the stitches will be angled toward their base, such as in the case of simple grass effects. Ensure the stitch completely covers the transfer line.

b Horizontal straight stitch (long)
This stitch is used in blocks to suggest landscape effects. Work *toward* any abutting groups of stitches. To suggest a break in perspective, void (see 4 below) between abutting fields. To blend shades within a single field, stitch into the abutting field.

c Free straight stitch (long or short)
Fine details, such as whiskers, do not appear as transferred pattern lines (see Basic Techniques, page 90). These can be worked freehand in straight stitches angled to suit the particular needs of the subject matter. Work *away* from abutting groups of stitches.

3 SHADOW LINING

Establish the direction of the imagined light source within your picture. Each element of the design away from this light source will be shadow lined. Put a pin in the work, its tip pointing in the direction of the light source, to remind you of its origin.

a Smooth shadow lining
Work a fine, accurate stem stitch along the pattern line, just to its underside.

b Fragmented shadow lining
Where a line is too irregular to permit shadow lining by stem stitch, use straight stitches tailored to the length of the section of outline to be described.

4 VOIDING

Where two fields of a filling technique abut (see below), with or without a shadow line, suggesting that one element of the design overlaps another, a narrow line void of stitching should be left between the two. In practice, this forms on the transferred pattern line dividing the two elements. It should be approximately as wide as the gauge of thread used for the embroidery itself. To check that the width is correct, loosely position a strand of the thread along the 'valley' of the void. If it fits snugly, the width is correct.

FILLING STITCHES

1 OPUS PLUMARIUM

This literally means feather work and emulates the way in which feathers lie smoothly, yet with infinite changes of direction, upon a bird's body. The angle of the stitches sweeps around without breaking the flow of the stitching itself and this in turn catches the light, refracting it back from the stitching and giving a three-dimensional impression.

a Radial opus plumarium
(single or first stratum)

Begin with a stitch central to the field to be covered. This, and all subsequent stitches, are worked from the *outer* edge of the transferred pattern line *inwards* toward the centre of the motif. Bring the needle out immediately adjacent to the top of the first stitch. Slip the needle beneath the first stitch and through the fabric about two-thirds of the way down

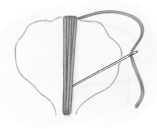

its length. This advances the angle of the stitching. Subsequent stitches can be either full length or shorter and angled as described, allowing the embroidery to fan out and cover the field without too many stitches 'bunching' at the inner core of the motif. A gradual advancement of the angle is achieved by working the angled stitches longer (e.g., three-quarters of the length of full stitches), more acute advancement of the angle by working them shorter (one quarter to half of the length of the full stitches).

b Radial opus plumarium
(subsequent strata)

Where a broad field of stitches is

required to fill a motif, several strata of *opus plumarium* may be required.

Work the first stratum by the single stratum method described above. Always stitching *inwards* (toward the core of the motif), work the second stratum by taking a first stitch at the centre of the field. Stitch into the first stratum (do not leave a void) and, following the established flow of the stitching, fan out on either side of the first stitch, advancing the angle when necessary, as before. Subsequent strata are worked similarly.

c Directional opus plumarium
(single or first stratum)

Where the core of the motif is elongated (such as the central vein of a simple elliptic leaf) the stitches should flow smoothly along its length. Again, always stitch inwards, bringing the needle out

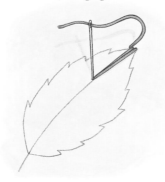

at the outer edge of the motif and in toward its centre.

Begin at the tip of the motif (or outer extremity of the first stratum) and take the first stitch inwards to abut the tip of the elongated core. Work your way down the field to be covered advancing the angle as necessary, as described above (a).

d Directional opus plumarium
(subsequent strata)

Work the first strata as described above. Again working from the direction of the

tip of the motif inwards, create subsequent strata by stitching into the previous stratum (do not void), advancing the angle of the stitching as necessary to match the abutting stitches.

2 OPPOSITE ANGLE STITCHING

This is used to create the effect of reflex, e.g., where a leaf or petal curls forward or backward to reveal its underside.

Following the principles of *opus plumarium* work the stitches at an exactly opposite angle to the abutting field. (Occasionally the angles will be similar in actuality, but opposite in relation to the concept of the directional stitching.) Where necessary void between the two.

3 SNAKE STITCH

This is used to describe long, sinuous shapes, such as broad blades of grass or other linear leaves.

a Simple snake stitch

Begin at the tip of the motif, taking the first stitch in the direction of the curve to be described. For subsequent stitches, bring the needle out on the *outside* of

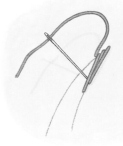

the curve and in on the *inside*. Work smoothly down the motif, advancing the angle of stitches, if necessary, by the *opus plumarium* method and lengthening the stitches where appropriate, as with graduating stem stitch (see above).

b Reflexing snake stitch

Begin at the point of reflex, where the direction of the curve changes. Firstly, take a stitch angled across the field slanting between the tip and base of the

curve. Work upwards to the tip, bringing the needle out on the outside of the curve and in on the inside until the upper field is complete. Advance the angle of stitching by the *opus plumarium* method if necessary. Complete the lower field by returning to the central stitch and working down the motif, again bringing the needle out on the outside and in on the inside of the curve. Advance the stitch angle as necessary.

4 DALMATIAN DOG TECHNIQUE

This is used to create a single, smooth field of embroidery where an area of one colour is completely encompassed by another colour. Used within *opus plumarium* (either radial or directional).

a Simple Dalmatian dog

Establish the radial or directional flow of the *opus plumarium*. Working the stitches at exactly the same angle as the main field of *opus plumarium* to follow,

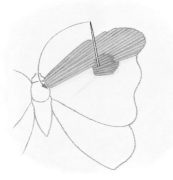

work the spots or other fields to be covered first. When completed, flood the rest of the *opus plumarium* around them, again paying careful attention to the flow of the stitches.

b Multiple Dalmatian dog

This technique can create a 'spot within a spot' or any other irregular pattern.

Establish either the radial or directional flow of the *opus plumarium*.

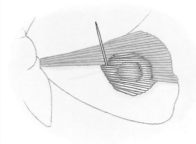

Maintaining the angle of stitching as above, work the innermost colour first, followed by outer field or fields of colour until the spots or other shapes are complete. Flood the surrounding *opus plumarium* around them.

DECORATIVE STITCHES

1 SEED STITCH

Fine, short, straight stitches worked directly onto the fabric, occasionally superimposed over other embroidery.

2 TICKING

These are seed stitches overlaying *opus plumarium*, worked at exactly the same angle as the underlying work but taken in the opposite direction, i.e., against the flow of the work.

3 STUDDING

These are seed stitches which overlay *opus plumarium*, but are worked at right angles to the underlying stitches.

4 SHOOTING STITCH

Long straight stitches taken in the opposite direction to the underlying radial or directional work.

5 CHEVRON STITCH

Two long straight stitches are angled to meet. Infill with a third straight stitch if necessary. To create a very sharp angle (such as a thistle spike) work a fourth straight stitch in a fine gauge of thread through the body of the motif.

6 DOTTING/SPECKLING

Work very short straight stitches, only as long as the width of the thread, to create an impression of tiny round dots. Work the stitches close together and in random directions.

7 FLOATING EMBROIDERY

This allows the threads to lie loosely on the fabric, falling into spontaneous shapes. Do not transfer the design to be formed onto the background fabric.

Take a long stitch from the inside to the outside of the motif, putting a finger or pencil under the thread to keep it away from the fabric. Take a very small stitch at the outer point of the motif to bring the thread back to the

surface. Take a third stitch back to the core of the motif, again keeping a finger beneath the thread. Repeat the process, removing the finger or pencil when several strands have built up.

8 SURFACE COUCHING

Usually a goldwork technique, this can be used effectively on various threads.

Bring the thread to be couched (the base thread) through the fabric to the surface of the work. If it is too thick to be brought through the fabric, lay it in place and hold it down with a thumb. Thread a second needle with a finer thread (the couching thread) and bring it up through the fabric immediately alongside the base thread. Take a tiny stitch over the base thread, at right angles to it, and repeat at regular intervals, effectively using the couching thread to whip the base thread into place along the transferred pattern line. Pay particular attention to whipping the beginning and the end of the base thread into place if it is lying wholly on the surface of the work.

9 SUBDUED VOIDING

Where two fields of *opus plumarium* abut and are separated by a voided line, the effect can be softened by working fine straight stitches, at the angle of the underlying work, across the void. Use a shade similar to that of the embroidered field 'closer' in perspective to the viewer, e.g., where a bird's wing lies over its body, or the angle of its neck creates a break in perspective. Work the overlying stitches at regular intervals, allowing the voided line to show through.

SUPPLIERS

There are many manufacturers and suppliers of embroidery materials and equipment and I have suggested a few here.
* This indicates suppliers who will accept orders direct from the given address via mail order.

Coats Crafts UK,
PO Box 22, The Lingfield Estate,
McMullen Road, Darlington,
Co. Durham DL1 1YQ, UK
Tel: 01325 365457
Stranded cottons

Coats and Clark,
Susan Bates Inc.,
30 Patewood Drive,
Greenville, SC 29615, USA
Tel: (US) 800 241 5997
Stranded cottons

DMC Creative World Ltd.,
Pullman Road, Wigston,
Leicestershire LE18 2DY, UK
Tel: 0116 281 1040
Fax: 0116 281 3592
Website: www.dmc/cw.com
Stranded cotton, imitation gold and
silver thread

DMC Corporation,
Building 10, Port Kearny,
South Kearny, NJ 07032, USA
Tel: (US) 201 589 0606
Stranded cotton, imitation gold and
silver thread

Japanese Embroidery Centre UK,*
White Lodge, Littlewick Road,
Lower Knaphill, Woking,
Surrey GU21 2JU, UK
Tel: 01483 476246
Floss silk, real gold and silver threads,
imitation gold, silver and coloured
metallic threads

Kreinik Manufacturing. Co., Inc.,
3106 Timanus Lane, Suite 101,
Baltimore, MD 21244, USA
Tel: (US) 800 537 2166
(UK ++01325 365 457)
Website: http://www.kreinik.com
E-mail: kreinik@kreinik.com
Blending filaments and metallic
threads

Madeira Threads (UK) Ltd.,
PO Box 6, Thirsk,
North Yorkshire YO7 3BX, UK
Tel: 01845 524880
E-mail: acts@madeira
Website: www.madeira.co.uk
Twisted/stranded silks

The Needlecraft Centre – Longleat, *
Stable Courtyard, Longleat,
Warminster,
Wiltshire BA12 7NL, UK
Tel: 01985 844774
General embroidery supplies

Pipers Specialist Silks, *
Chinnerys, Egremont Street,
Glemsford, Sudbury,
Suffolk CI10 7SA, UK
Tel: 01787 280920
Website: http://www.pipers-silks.com
E-mail: susanpeck@pipers-silks.com
Floss and spun (twisted) silk. Exclusive silk
kits designed by Helen M. Stevens

Stephen Simpson Ltd., *
50 Manchester Road,
Preston PR1 3YH, UK
Tel: 01772 556688
Real gold and silver threads

The Voirrey Embroidery Centre, *
Brimstage Hall,
Wirral L63 6JA, UK
Tel: 0151 3423514
General embroidery supplies

Helen M. Stevens
(Enquiries via David & Charles or website
below)
Website: www.helenmstevens.co.uk
For embroidery masterclass tutorials,
lectures and commissions

ACKNOWLEDGEMENTS

Many thanks, as ever, to the team at David and Charles for their help in creating this new concept of embroidery book.
Nigel Salmon deserves particular praise for his tireless efforts to capture silk in the medium of photography – and he has succeeded!
A number of the embroideries in this book appear courtesy of my clients. Thank you all. . .

Plate 1	Martha Van Koevering		Plate 22	Mrs. S. Greenwood
Plate 2	Mrs. L. R. Hazell		Plate 23	Susan Adamson
Plate 8	Mrs. J. Taylor Balls		Plate 27	Lesley Godwin
Plate 14	Mrs. Margaret Brown		Plate 28	Mrs. Joan Hipwood
Plate 17	John and Bridget Collins		Plate 29	Sue Narramore

Plates 4 and 18 first appeared in *Needlecraft* Magazine, published by Future Publishing.

INDEX

FLOWERS

Italic page numbers indicate plates; **bold** page numbers indicate figures.

Acanthus 5
Anemone *28*, *29*
Antirrhinum 7, **7**
Arrowhead 77–8, *78*

Bindweed *41*, 42–3, 48–55
Bittersweet *57*, 58
Bluebell 57, 62–9, 77
Bramble (blackberry) 59, *60*
Bryony *5*, **42**
Bulrush 77
Bur-reed 79–83, 86–7
Buttercup 9, 12, **12**, *13*

Clover 9, 10, **10**, *13*
Columbine 63, **63**
Comfrey 75, **76**
Common restharrow 45, *45*

Corncockle 10, *11*
Cornflower 9, 10, *11*
Corn marigold 9, *9*
Cow parsley 43–4, *43*
Cowslip 45, **45**
Cranesbill 26, 30–1
    meadow *41*, 42

Dandelion 73–4, *73*
Duckweed *73*

Evening primrose 26, 29–30, **31**, 32–8, *32*

Flowering rush 79–83, 85–6
Foxglove 25–6, *25*
Fuchsia 26, 29, *29*

Geranium
    see Cranesbill
Grasses 31, 45, *45*, 77
Great mullein *41*, 42

Hawthorn 43
Helleborines 57, **58**
Herb Robert *28*, 30–1, 32–9, *32*, 42
Holly 5
Hollyhock 26, **28**
Honeysuckle **7**, 59–60, *61*
Hop **42**

Ivy *5*

Lily 5
Lords and ladies 59, 62–7, **62**, 71
Lucerne 10, **10**

Mallow 5, 13–14, **14**, 16–23
Mock orange 25, *25*
Morning glory 26

Nasturtium 25, *25*
Night-scented stock **31**

Orchid 57, **58**
    early purple *57*, 59
    lady's slipper 62, *63*
Pelargonium **30**
Periwinkle, lesser 60, *61*
Petunia 26
Plantain *41*, 42–3, **44**
Polyanthus 25, *25*
Poppy 5, 7, 9, *11*, **12**, 13–14, 16–23
Primrose 77

Ragged robin *57*, 59
Rose 5, *5*, 25, *25*

Scarlet pimpernel *57*, 58
Silverweed *41*, 42
Snowdrop 5
Spotted medick 10, *10*
St John's wort 15
Sweet pea 5–6, **6**, 26, *27*, 28
Sweet violet 5, 62, 64–7, 69–70

Thistle 9, 12, **12**, *13*, *15*, 45–6, *46*
Tobacco plant 25, *25*, **31**
Traveller's joy *57*, 58, **59**
Tutsan 15

Vetch 6, **6**

Water-crowfoot 73, *73*
Water forget-me-not 75–6
Water lily 73, *73*, 74, **74**
Water plantain *73*, 74
Water violet 74–6, *75*
Wild strawberry *57*, 58
Willowherb 46–55, **47**, *79*
Windflower *28*, 29
Winter aconite 5
Wood-sorrel 62, 64–7, 70

Yellow archangel *57*, 59
Yellow flag iris 78, 79–85
Yellow pimpernel *57*, 58

STITCHES AND TECHNIQUES

Chevron stitch 94

Dalmatian dog technique 94
    multiple 94
    simple 94
Dotting/speckling 94

Fabric 88
Floating embroidery 94

Mounting fabric (in tambour hoop) 91

Opposite angle stitching 93
Opus plumarium 92–3
    directional 93
    radial 93

Presentation (mounting and framing) 91

Seed stitch 94
Shadow lining 92
    fragmented 92
    smooth 92
Shooting stitch 94

Snake stitch 93
    reflexing 93
    simple 93
Stem stitch 92
    broad 92
    coiling 92
    fine/narrow 92
    graduating 92
    reflexing 92
Straight stitch 92
    free 92
    horizontal 92
    vertical 92

Studding 94
Subdued voiding 94
Surface couching 94

Threads 88
    blending filaments 89
    cotton 88
    floss silk 88
    'real' gold and silver thread 89
    synthetic metallic threads 88
    twisted silk 88

Ticking 94
Tools 89
    embroidery frame 89
    needles 89
    scissors 89
Transferring a design 90

Voiding 92